I'm Nobody!
Who Are You?

I'm Nobody!
Who Are You?

THE STORY OF EMILY DICKINSON

by Edna Barth

drawings by Richard Cuffari

CLARION BOOKS

TICKNOR & FIELDS: A HOUGHTON MIFFLIN COMPANY

NEW YORK

Acknowledgments

Poetry on pages 45, 46, 53, 81, 92, 98, 107, 111 reprinted by permission of the publishers and the Trustees of Amherst College from Thomas H. Johnson, Editor, *The Poems of Emily Dickinson*, Cambridge, Mass.: The Belknap Press of Harvard University Press, Copyright 1951, 1955 by The President and Fellows of Harvard College.

Short excerpts from the letters reprinted by permission of the publishers from Thomas H. Johnson, Editor, *The Letters of Emily Dickinson*, Cambridge, Mass.: Harvard University Press, Copyright 1958, by The President and Fellows of Harvard College.

Emily Dickinson's spelling, punctuation, and capitalization, retained by Mr. Johnson in the poems and letters, remain intact in this book.

Clarion Books
Ticknor & Fields, a Houghton Mifflin Company

Designed by Judith Lerner
Printed in the U.S.A.

Library of Congress Catalog Card Number: 72-129211
ISBN 0-395-28843-6
(previously published by The Seabury Press under ISBN 0-8164-3029-2)
V   10   9   8   7

to Emily,
the grandmother
I loved but never knew

Author's Note

MY NEW ENGLAND grandmother, also named Emily, and dead long before I was born, was a contemporary of Emily Dickinson. A trunk in our attic held several notebooks of her own delicate though undistinguished verse—one of my few means of bringing her alive.

In Amherst, Massachusetts, where I first worked as a librarian, I found the spirit of Emily Dickinson very much alive. The house behind the hemlock hedges, where she had lived and died so quietly, was pointed out to me at once. People connected with her in one way or another came into the library. The Reverend Mr. and Mrs. Hervey Parke, who then owned and occupied the Dickinson house with several sons and a daughter, kindly invited me to dinner and a "sing" afterward in the back parlor.

Always fond of poetry, I had a preference for Keats, Shelley, and other poets of the British Romantic Movement. Now I discovered the poet who saw "New Englandly," as Emily Dickinson said herself—the poet who saw the vital implications of the small commonplaces of

7

life, who said so much in so few words, and who, above all, never tried to be anything but herself.

Having missed so much by not encountering Emily Dickinson in my own early years, I have written this book for children. I hope it will convey to them something of Emily Dickinson, as a poet and as a person.

Every incident or conversation in the book either actually took place or is based on recorded facts of the poet's life. The poems speak for themselves.

EDNA BARTH
March, 1971

Contents

	Author's Note	7
1	DEAR MARCH, COME IN!	13
2	GOBLINS	17
3	THE STILE OF PEARL	23
4	I DON'T BELIEVE I AM 17	30
5	WE INTRODUCE OURSELVES TO PLANETS AND TO FLOWERS	40
6	I STARTED EARLY—TOOK MY DOG—	49
7	THE SOUL SELECTS HER OWN SOCIETY	58
8	BAREFOOT RANK	65
9	I'M NOBODY! WHO ARE YOU?	72
10	I KNOW THAT IS POETRY	76
11	SUCCESS IS COUNTED SWEETEST	80
12	THE POETS LIGHT BUT LAMPS	87
	Selected Poems by Emily Dickinson	95
	For Further Reading	121
	Sources	123
	Index of Poems by First Lines	125
	General Index	127

I'm Nobody!
Who Are You?

I · *Dear March, Come In!*

IT WAS ONLY the first of March, but the moment Emily opened her eyes that morning, she knew spring had come. Where the heavy curtain panels met at the middle, sunlight came pouring through. And there was something different about it.

Jumping down from her high bed, she ran to the window and pulled the curtains apart.

Snow still partly covered the lawn below, and lay in icy circles around the trunks of elm and fir trees. But the sky had a new brightness.

Careful not to wake her sister Lavinia, Emily wriggled into her clothes, crept downstairs, and out the back door.

She was right! Spring *was* arriving. At the sunny southeast corner of the house, the earth had humped up into tiny hills, broken open at the top. Down inside were clusters of plump yellow-green crocus shoots.

"Austin, Austin," Emily called softly, hoping her older brother might look out. If Father heard her, he would scold. Out here in the March wind with only a light shawl around her shoulders, a girl who had spent so much time sick in bed the winter before!

The barn was noisy with the stomping of horses and there were all sorts of squealing and scampering sounds. In the henhouse the birds cluck-clucked and shook their feathers. Now and then a rooster crowed.

The sounds were all part of Emily Dickinson's life in the family homestead in Amherst, Massachusetts. A man named Deacon Mack owned and lived in half of the large brick house, and Emily's father had just sold him the other half. Now he could buy his family a whole house of their own.

"It will be so lovely," Emily's mother said nearly every day. "Not sharing a roof with another family!"

Emily was excited about it, too, but she had been born here, and this was home. How could another place be quite the same? As she stood thinking about it, the back door opened and shut with a loud bang, and Lavinia came running out.

"Emily, what are you doing out here? It's time for prayers, and Father's so vexed."

Lavinia stood on a little rise, keeping her boots dry. She was younger than Emily but often seemed to be looking after her.

"Oh, Vinnie, I forgot." As they ran in, Emily told her about the crocuses.

The year was 1840. Emily was nine years old. Lavinia was seven, and their brother Austin eleven.

In the parlor Father sat, tall and stern, the opened Bible

on his lap. His lips met in a narrow line. His brown eyes, between his side whiskers, seemed to see nothing as the two girls took their seats. But Emily knew that, like God, he saw everything. That surely included the bedraggled skirts and muddy boots of his older daughter.

The clock on the marble mantel ticked loudly; its brass pendulum swung back and forth, back and forth. Emily was positive that the thumping of her own heart was much louder.

"Emily," Father said suddenly, as if he could read her very thoughts, "what time is it?"

Emily's heart pounded harder than ever. She looked in misery at the hands of the clock.

One day long before, Father had taken her into the parlor to teach her to tell time. "Do you understand?" he had asked at the end. Afraid to say No, Emily had nodded as if she understood. She still could not tell time.

Now, as Father gazed at her sternly, she mumbled, "Late, Father."

Austin started to grin, then stopped. From his place beside Father, he sent a message of sympathy across the room. Mother sat in sad-faced disapproval, her hands folded in her lap. Vinnie's brown eyes were solemn.

"I'll talk to you later, Emily," Father said. Then he opened the Bible to the Book of Revelation to read the chapter for today.

The words made vivid pictures in Emily's mind. There were fiery dragons, and a serpent who was really the devil. There were beings in white robes—whether angels or people, she didn't know. One beautiful creature had the sun as her clothing and a crown made of twelve of the stars.

After Father closed the Bible, they all knelt on the carpet for prayers.

But Emily was still caught up in the strangely beautiful images of the verses from Revelation. They half frightened her but, at the same time, sent tingles of pleasure along her spine. For the moment she forgot about the scolding and punishment that lay ahead.

2 · *Goblins*

EVERYTHING in the Dickinson homestead seemed to be standing on its head. Pictures were piled on the floor. The legs of tables and chairs stuck into the air. Carpets leaned against the walls, in tall rolls.

Father strode through the rooms, pointing, directing. The moving men passed in and out. In the drive, patient farm horses waited for the wagons to be loaded.

Busy as Austin was supposed to be, helping the men, he found time to ruffle Vinnie's hair and give Emily's apron sash a tug. "No dawdling, young ladies." His brown eyes were bright with excitement. Father had just told him he could have a stand of pine out behind the grape arbors at the new place.

"Vinnie, you must keep this kitten from underfoot." Mother, usually quite placid, sounded cross. "And Emily, what are you doing there at the window? You were told to wrap up these cups."

Emily was saying good-bye—to the forsythia, now in brilliant yellow blossom, and to everything else, but she could never tell Mother a thing like that.

"Come, Emily," Mother said more crossly still. "There's plenty of forsythia at the Pleasant Street house. And just think, girls"—her tone changed and her blue eyes lit up—"a pump right at the kitchen sink!"

An hour later she and her two daughters set out for their new home. The spring muds had dried early and the road was solid under their feet. As soon as the village green came in sight, Emily and Vinnie went skipping ahead.

A few buggies and farm wagons were already tied to the rail fence. Part pasture, part swamp, the green was the center of the town. Rough dirt roads led in from the countryside all around.

The girls ran as far as the post office where the yellow mail coach pulled in every day. Looking back, they saw Mother frown and shake her head. The windows of Father's law office gazed down at them from above a store. They were supposed to walk sedately like Mother. Weren't they young ladies, and Dickinsons besides?

From where they stood they could see their church, south of the village green, and beyond that the buildings of Amherst College, which seemed almost to belong to them. Grandfather Dickinson had helped found it, and their father was its present treasurer. Oh, Father was very important—to the college, to the town, and even to the state. For two years he had served in the Massachusetts General Court.

Turning north, the Dickinsons walked up Pleasant Street. "There it is!" Vinnie cried out. "There's *our* house." She and Emily began running again.

It was a solid white wooden house with one huge central chimney on top. The houses of neighbors pressed close, but there was a big front lawn and plenty of room at the back.

Emily and Vinnie went running up and downstairs, their voices echoing through the empty rooms. In the bedroom they were going to share, Vinnie came to an abrupt halt. "The bed ought to go here," she said. "Your chest over there, Emily, and mine here."

"Well—perhaps," Emily half agreed.

They peeped into every cupboard and closet, and out of every window. Across the way was the district schoolhouse where they had both learned to read and write.

Next, they went out to the orchard to inspect the apple trees, some with trunks as big around as the trunks of elms. They ran into the barn, up to the hayloft, and back down.

Outside again in the April sunshine, the excitement ebbing, Emily had a sudden feeling of alarm. Home seemed to have disappeared. Where was it? Behind the gaping windows of the white house? In those echoing rooms? No! But home was not back at the homestead, either. There everything had been topsy-turvy for days.

She reached out for Vinnie's hand. "Let's go out to the road now and see if Austin's coming." He was to ride with Father on the first wagonload of furniture. With Austin and Father there, the feeling of strangeness might go away.

In a few days the white house did seem less strange. Mother bustled cheerfully about, unaware that anyone in her family could be less than perfectly happy. Every morning Father went out the door in his black broadcloth clothes and gray beaver hat, as he always had.

All around were the same fields and wooded hills Emily had always known. She spent hours in the woods, looking for lady-slippers, trillium, and eerie white-stemmed Indian pipes, sometimes with Vinnie and other girls, but often by herself.

One day she and Vinnie found a spot that was like a little room, with the scraggly lower branches of some old pines for walls. The next morning Emily went back alone. Overnight a whole colony of mushrooms had sprung up out of a spongy bed of brown pine needles. Like elves, Emily thought, storing the sight of them away in her imagination. Years later she would write:

> *The Mushroom is the Elf of Plants—*
> *At Evening he is not—*
> *At Morning, in a Truffled Hut*
> *It stop upon a Spot*
>
> (first stanza)

In a little while she pushed on, through the brush, now and then squashing a puff ball with her foot to hear it pop.

Suddenly an angry mother bird flew out of a thicket. With loud chirps, she fluttered back and forth across the path.

She doesn't want me to know where her nest is, Emily thought, walking on. She is keeping her babies safe. "Don't fret," she said softly to the mother bird.

The pine fragrance disappeared, and a dank odor took its place. There was a swamp ahead. Perhaps she would come upon one of the red cardinal flowers that were so hard to find.

Emily looked carefully through the tall grass at the edge of the swamp. There were no flowers there at all. Then she saw one—a red spot way over at the other side. She would have to wade across to get it.

She shivered, for the first time a little frightened. Hadn't her mother warned her to keep away from the swamps? "Why, a snake might bite you," she had said. Snakes—or goblins, Emily thought.

She took a deep breath and started across. The mud tugged at her shoes, and one shoe came off. But not until the red flower was in her hand did she go back.

"Emily," her mother scolded when she came home with burrs clinging to her skirts and her shoes muddy. "How can you be so disobedient? You know Father and I don't want you off in the woods alone." She looked at the rare flower in Emily's hand, and shook her head.

"I suppose I shouldn't have," Emily admitted, looking seriously into her mother's face. But dancing through her mind were pictures of the wonderful things she had seen.

On the fourth of July the first green peas from the new garden appeared on the dinner table. In August there was summer squash. By Thanksgiving the cellar was bulging with barrels of potatoes, turnips, carrots, apples, and winter pears. The pantry shelves and the cellarway were lined with jars of preserves. Firewood for the winter reached nearly to the shed rafters. "The highest woodpile in town!" Austin boasted.

The Dickinsons were ready for the long Amherst winter. And they were all together as they always had been. And always would be. Emily, at least, could not picture the family as ever separating.

3 · *The Stile of Pearl*

"GOOD-BYE, Austin, good-bye!" Emily and Vinnie were both crying as they waved.

In the carriage beside Father, Austin grinned and waved back. Not quite thirteen, he was off for the spring term at Williston Seminary for "improvement." And the worst of it was that Austin seemed to want to go. He preferred a schoolful of strange boys, ten miles from home, to Emily—and the rest of the family.

"Be sure to send your clothes home for mending by anybody who is coming this way, Austin," Mother called out as the horse trotted down the drive. "He seems so young to be leaving home," she said with a catch in her voice.

Why did she *let* him? Emily wondered resentfully. Why didn't she stand up to Father?

Much as she missed Austin, Emily was soon writing him cheerful letters. She told him how many eggs the hens had laid, who had taken tea at the Dickinsons' lately, and which teachers had returned for the spring term at Amherst Academy.

She and Vinnie went to school there now. Every morning they set out with their arms full of books for the three-story brick academy building, a short walk from home. Grandfather Dickinson had helped found it, as he had the college, and Father had gone to school there himself.

Emily and her brother and sister were fortunate, their father said. Plenty of children their age had to go out to work or stay home on their fathers' farms to help. He told them to be good, to work hard, and to learn all they could. Then when they grew up, they could teach others to do right.

Reading for pleasure was a waste of time, he said. Any spare moments should be spent reading the Bible. This had been hammered into the children all their lives, but Austin and Emily read books by Charles Dickens and any other stories they could lay their hands on. They talked them over in secret and hid them from Father, under the piano cover or in the syringa bush by the front door. Emily was going to miss this now that Austin was gone.

But her studies and her new friends at Amherst Academy were beginning to absorb her. Expressing oneself well in written and oral language had equal or greater importance at that time than ability in mathematics and science. And Emily liked to write. She was soon turning out humorous articles and stories for the school paper, as well as compositions of outstanding originality.

Every scene she described was vivid and real. Every person came to life. To Emily, words themselves seemed to be alive. This is the way she put it herself when she was grown up:

> *A word is dead*
> *When it is said,*
> *Some say.*
> *I say it just*
> *Begins to live*
> *That day.*

Each Wednesday afternoon a number of pupils were assigned to read their compositions to the whole school. And though Emily loved to put her ideas on paper, she dreaded standing up before the others to read them aloud. Even walking into the assembly hall after everyone was seated was a painful ordeal.

"Wait till *you* have to do it," she said to Vinnie.

"I shall like it," Vinnie declared. "I shan't be one bit afraid."

Emily looked admiringly at her nine-year-old sister who was so different from herself. Though they squabbled sometimes, Emily would not have exchanged her for any sister in the world.

One Wednesday Emily took her seat in the hall early. As the benches around her filled, she felt more and more fearful. Up front on the platform sat a row of teachers. How would she ever stand up there when her turn came? The hand holding her composition papers began to tremble.

Walking into the room just then was a girl she had

never seen before. There was a merry look in her eyes. Bright curls framed her face. As she came down the aisle, Emily looked at her closely. Could those be dandelion blossoms pinned to her hair like yellow curls? They were!

Emily began to smile. For a few minutes, the feeling of dread went away.

The girl who had dared to walk into the assembly with dandelion curls was Abiah Root from West Springfield, Massachusetts. For many boys and girls from other towns came to the academy, boarding with friends or relatives and sometimes staying only for a term or two.

Abiah and Emily were soon best friends and the center of a small circle of others. Emily had a startling way, the girls found, of saying things other people merely thought. And she could send them into gales of laughter with comical tales made up on the spot.

Emily loved and worshiped her teachers as she did her friends. Warmth and closeness were something she had always hungered for at home. Father kept his feelings so hidden, and Mother, though less awesome, was no better at showing affection. Austin was away, and Vinnie was so young.

While Abiah Root was in Amherst she and Emily exchanged secrets and private jokes, and had long heart-to-heart talks. Then, after two terms, Abiah announced that her parents were transferring her to a school near her own home.

"Promise that you will write to me often and come to visit me," Emily begged. "You know you're my dearest friend, Abiah, and always will be." When Emily loved anyone, she loved with all her might.

Letters were soon flying back and forth between Amherst and Springfield. Tucked within the pages were pressed flowers and sometimes a lock snipped from the girls' own hair.

On and off for the next six years Emily and Vinnie went to classes at the academy. There Emily was happy learning Latin, mathematics, history, and sciences. Botany taught her more about the plants and flowers she loved. Even more wonderful were the plays and poems of William Shakespeare.

At fourteen, she was still small, a rather pale girl with large wondering brown eyes and thick glossy chestnut hair.

"This term you had better not confine yourself at school," her mother said, worried. "You need exercise. Besides, Emily, it's high time you learned to bake bread." The winter before Emily had had influenza, followed by a lingering cough. It was autumn now, and she was coughing again.

A cough that lingered could mean tuberculosis, fever the beginning of diphtheria, typhoid or scarlet fever. Penicillin and other modern medicines were unknown. Many people died while they were children or in their teens.

Every funeral procession passed along Pleasant Street. At the Dickinson house Emily and Vinnie, their faces pressed to the window, watched the sad-eyed people and the wagon bearing the coffin. Emily thought a long time about the person who had died, especially if it was someone she knew. And she thought of all the others lying under stones in the cemetery.

When she was little, people she knew had sometimes disappeared. No one had told her where they went. Now she knew, of course—where their bodies went, at least. But what about their souls?

If they had lived good lives, they were in heaven. If they had not, they were being punished—a punishment that went on forever. This was what the minister preached each Sabbath at long morning and afternoon meetings, and what most people seemed to believe.

Though the Dickinsons attended this Orthodox Congregational church regularly, they were not members. Membership called for a public declaration of faith that went against their reticent nature.

When Emily was fifteen, a revival of religious fervor swept through the town and college. With her family she attended some of the revival meetings.

"If you die tomorrow," a visiting preacher would thunder, "will you rise to a life of glory in heaven, or go down to eternal punishment?"

As fear ran through the rows of benches, Emily listened and shivered.

"All men are born sinners. Before it is too late, confess your guilt and be forgiven. Stand up. Declare yourself a true Christian!"

Night after night the meetings went on. And, one after another, people of all ages arose. Many were friends or relatives of the Dickinsons. After they had declared themselves, Emily noticed, a change came over them.

One of the preachers explained how it happened. A

person undergoing conversion discovered, with a shock, how deeply sinful he was. Then, as he thought about it, gloom would set in. Next came an intense inner struggle, and finally a feeling of release and ecstasy. Like everyone else, Emily was caught up in the fervor, but the state of ecstasy she was longing for never came.

Her father was certainly a good and righteous man, but he had never risen to declare his faith. Father, though, was an adult, and Emily was more concerned with people of her own age. So many girls in town had already been converted. Abiah, in Springfield, was very close to it.

What made Emily so different? She didn't know, and it troubled her. A converted Christian was supposed to fear God, his life on earth just a preparation for life thereafter. But life on earth was beautiful. It was filled with trees, flowers and birds, mountains and streams, sunsets and stars, with one's family and friends.

"I have tried but I can't give up the world," Emily told a friend, "even if it is the only way of getting to heaven." Wistfully, years later, she wrote in the last two stanzas of a poem:

> Perhaps the "Kingdom of Heaven's" changed—
> I hope the "Children" there
> Won't be "new fashioned" when I come—
> And laugh at me—and stare—
>
> I hope the Father in the skies
> Will lift his little girl,—
> Old fashioned, naughty, everything,—
> Over the stile of "Pearl."

4 · I Don't Believe I Am 17

EDWARD DICKINSON believed it was good for young people to go to school away from home for a time. The autumn Emily was sixteen, her turn came. She was to attend Mount Holyoke Female Seminary in South Hadley, ten miles away.

The students were not all from New England by any means. "I've heard tell that some of them are from New York," Vinnie said. "And some from way down South."

"It's true," Emily said.

Would such girls be friendly or not? As Edward Dickinson's daughter, she could expect respect, but would they like her? With a little toss of her head, she said, "They're an unmannerly lot—some of them, or so I've heard."

Vinnie nodded. "I've heard that, too."

Emily sat thinking. Ever since she had heard of Mount Holyoke, with its reputation for high academic standards, she had been eager to go. But now, she was having doubts. "Oh, Vinnie," she burst out, "how shall I ever get along without you?"

"I shall write to you and come and visit you," Vinnie promised. "And you'll have cousin Emily." Emily Norcross was in her final year at the seminary, and she and Emily Dickinson were to share a room.

"And just think, Emily," Vinnie went on in a tone of awe, "you'll be studying under Miss Mary Lyon."

She had touched one of Emily's buried fears. Miss Mary Lyon, the founder and principal of the seminary, was known for the religious training she gave her students as well as an excellent general education. Many became "true Christians." What would happen, Emily wondered, to a student who refused?

By September, fear of the difficult entrance examinations loomed largest. Failure would mean being sent home in disgrace.

"Oh, you'll pass, Em," Austin assured her seriously. He was proud of his sister's brilliance. Then, as usual, he began to tease. "Just mind your P's and Q's, and try not to collide with the she-dragon." Austin was in Amherst College now, busy with his own studies and his new friends. He promised to drive over and see her whenever he could.

Tearful good-byes from her mother and Vinnie did little to cheer Emily the morning she left home. White-faced and stiff, she sat in the buggy beside her silent father.

The road to South Hadley wound through a notch in the mountains, emerging at last from thick woods. Yellowed fields sloped gently down toward the little village. And there, in full sight, was the five-story brick seminary building.

Emily began to cough. Excitement had kept her awake most of the night before, and she felt suddenly exhausted.

Her father glanced at her once, then looked quickly away.

Will he miss me? Emily wondered. On her father's face as he pulled into the seminary drive, there was no trace of what he may have felt. He helped Emily down from the buggy, picked up one of her bags, and strode with firm steps toward the door.

A smiling student answered their knock, and they caught glimpses of others inside. A moment later in the seminary parlor, Emily was face to face with Miss Mary Lyon herself.

To Emily's relief, she was excused from taking the entrance examinations until the following day. There would be time to unpack and rest, and to look about her.

"It is natural for a girl leaving home for the first time to be a little homesick," Miss Lyon told her in a kindly tone. "I have always believed, though," she went on, "that people who give in to homesickness lack character." Her keen blue eyes seemed to bore deep into Emily's soul.

With no trouble at all, Emily passed the entrance examinations and was put into the youngest class. At the end of the term, if she did well, she would go into the middle class.

From six in the morning, when the girls rose, to the bell for lights out at nine forty-five P.M., each day was packed full. Emily went to chapel, studied, recited, practiced the piano, sang in the choir, exercised in a calisthenics class, and did dining hall duty. She helped her cousin care for their little room, and she washed, ironed, and mended her own clothes.

"I try not to be homesick," she told her cousin one night after they were both in bed. "I'm afraid I must be lacking in character."

Lectures by Miss Lyon on sin, on death, and on the life after death were a part of each seminary day. The term had hardly begun when she called the students together. Each girl was to rise when her name was called and say whether or not she had hope of becoming a true Christian.

The teacher who recorded their answers wrote beside the name Emily Dickinson the words "no hope."

Mary Lyon told of her own sudden blinding revelation out of doors in the Buckland Hills. From that day on she had dedicated her life to God. Emily was waiting for the same sort of revelation, but it never came, and she was too honest to pretend.

Other meetings followed and from each one Emily came away more disturbed.

Six weeks passed, a longer time than she ever had been away from home. In a letter to her friend Abiah she tried to pretend that all was well.

"I am now contented and happy," she said, "if I can be happy when absent from my dear home and friends. You may laugh at the idea, but you must remember that I have a very dear home."

Among the youngest to enter the seminary that year,

Emily passed a difficult geometry examination, completed history and English grammar courses, and wrote a number of brilliant compositions.

She had made some friends now, and she entertained them at recess with pungent comments and comical stories made up as she went along. Some of her ways were strange, though, the girls found.

"Emily," two of her new friends called out one day. "Where are you going? Didn't you hear about the menagerie? It is going to stop out front, and we're all to be excused from classes to watch the monkeys and dancing bears. What! You're not coming?"

Emily shook her head No, and instead slipped away from the seminary to the woods. Colored leaves floated like tiny ships on the surface of a little stream. A rabbit scurried off into the underbrush in fright. Then the screen of trees above gave way to blue sky, and she was on an open slope. Harvested fields rolled off in gentle waves toward hills ablaze with red and gold, orange and russet. The air was fragrant with sun-warmed grasses, leaves, and pine needles.

For a moment the world seemed perfect. Heaven must be like this, Emily thought, not the heaven of the "true Christian" but the one she was seeking herself.

On her way back she picked a few perfectly shaped bright red maple leaves.

"They *are* pretty," her cousin remarked when she saw them on Emily's nightstand. "I saw you coming across the cornfield today. So that's where you were—off in the woods—by yourself." She looked curiously at her younger cousin.

To Emily it was the others who were strange. Preferring a menagerie to this unexpected chance for a bit of privacy! Ten years later she wrote this poem:

The Show is not the Show
But they that go—
Menagerie to me
My neighbor be—
Fair Play—
Both went to see—

Since the beginning of the term, Emily had been counting the days until the Thanksgiving holiday. The day before she was up long before the usual time, rousing her cousin, who was to go with her.

"We must be *ready*," she said, though Austin would not call for them until nearly noon. For hours she waited impatiently at a window, peering through a driving rain for a glimpse of the carriage, until at last Austin was there.

Rain still fell in torrents and a wild wind tossed the branches of the leafless elms when the spires and rooftops of Amherst came in sight. To Emily the town had never looked lovelier.

At the Dickinsons' door Mother, Father, and Vinnie stood in a welcoming group, Mother with tears in her eyes.

In a glowing letter to Abiah, Emily described the days that followed—the big Thanksgiving dinner, the callers who came, and the fun she and her cousin had with other young people in the evening, playing games and enjoying a "candy scrape."

On Monday, back at the seminary, homesickness descended again. But Emily was soon lost in her studies and as content as she could be away from home.

In a letter to Austin, written on December 11, 1847, the day after her birthday, she said, "I don't believe I am 17." Like others of her age, Emily was trying to find out what she really felt and thought. Of one thing she was certain. She felt safest and happiest under her father's roof, with Austin and Vinnie nearby.

Christmas would be observed in traditional Puritan style. Making a holiday of it was considered pagan. The girls would stay on campus, as did most New England college students.

On December 24, a hush fell over the whole seminary. Many of the students fasted. A few days later Miss Lyon held another important prayer meeting. No girl was ever forced to undergo religious conversion. Nevertheless the head mistress made it clear that, in her eyes, no other path was right.

"Are you prepared to do what no one else is willing to do?" she asked in low forceful tones. "Are you willing to go where no one else will go?" She was proud of former students who were now missionaries in Turkey, Persia, India, China, and the Sandwich Islands. If others followed, she would be prouder still.

Emily frowned. How would she spend *her* life—as a teacher or missionary? Never. The thought of exposing herself to so many people was unbearable.

Then she thought of her mother, completely content as the mistress of the household. Wasn't there something more? Suddenly restless and dissatisfied, she looked at her name on her copybook—the same name as Mother's. Perhaps she should start spelling it Emilie.

Still among the students with no hope, Emily had seen them leave, one by one, to join the other group. She knew that letters about her were passing among her aunts and cousins and that Emily Norcross had begun to pray for her. And she knew, too, how much she was disappointing her teachers. Miss Whitman had gone so far as to tell her what a pity it was that such an excellent student should be so willful and rebellious.

Emily made a joke of it in letters to Austin and Vinnie, but inside she was deeply shaken.

At last an evening came when all but one in the group without hope rose to their feet. Emily sat as if made of stone.

"They thought it queer that I didn't rise," she explained to a friend later. "I thought it would be queerer to tell a lie."

The inner struggle went on, until a Sunday in mid-January, when she woke with an odd feeling that this day would prove crucial. A popular minister named Mr. Blodgett preached two sermons in the seminary chapel, and Emily was strangely moved. At last she, too, felt almost ready to dedicate herself. Miss Lyon was so inspired herself that she spoke with special fervor at a meeting in the afternoon. With sixteen others Emily went in the evening to a private meeting with the headmistress. There, kneeling on Miss Lyon's carpet, she came the closest she ever had to conversion.

Four days later the winter vacation began, with two

glorious weeks at home. The spell was broken. Any "hope" Emily had had was gone, and with it any enthusiasm for Mount Holyoke Seminary.

But Father had sent her here to study, so study she would, in spite of the fact that she was not planning to return the following year.

"You must not expect to hear from me often," she wrote to Austin, "for I have but little time to write, but you must write to me as often as possible."

In their room under the eaves, Emily and her cousin stuffed their little stove with wood at night, but by morning they found a layer of ice in the water pitcher.

For days Emily had walked around as if carrying a tremendous weight, hardly able to mount the stairs. Then one bitterly cold morning she woke up with chills and fever.

Emily Norcross took one look at her and said, "Stay in bed." She threw kindling into the stove and started a fire. After breakfast she brought up gruel and tea and a hot flatiron wrapped in flannel for Emily's bed.

Miss Lyon sent a young teacher up, and later on came up herself. "Don't fret," she told Emily. "We'll call the doctor." Then, she knelt by the bed and prayed—for Emily's bodily health and for her soul.

All her life Emily had had the approval of her teachers. To have lost it here at the seminary sent her into a state of despair. Long after she was well and out of bed, gloom hung over her. A hacking cough kept her awake at night. She grew thinner and thinner.

"Home was always dear to me, and dearer still the

friends around it," she wrote to Austin, "but never did it seem so dear as now."

Toward the end of March, the news reached Amherst that Emily was in poor health, and Austin was sent over to take her home.

"Before the close of the term?" Emily protested, determined to complete at least her year. "To be dosed with Father's medicines and have all the old ladies in town calling me 'poor child.'" She began to cry. "I shan't go."

But Father's word was law. Emily went home, keeping up with her classes on her own, and returning only for the final term, which ended in August.

5 · We Introduce Ourselves to Planets and to Flowers

EMILY's education was over. Like other unmarried daughters of well-to-do families, she was expected to live at home with her parents, doing her share of the household duties, until a suitable husband came along.

The young men who took Emily and Vinnie on sleigh rides or for drives in buggies were classmates of Austin's, college instructors, and apprentices from their father's law office. Sometimes they gathered in the Dickinsons' parlor, the chatter and laughter halting abruptly when awesome Mr. Dickinson walked in. Father Dickinson kept a sharp eye on his daughters' callers; Mrs. Dickinson had the irritating habit of asking them over and over if they were warm enough or would like another piece of cake. Emily was always relieved when her parents left.

"But what good times we are having," Vinnie said one night as she and Emily got ready for bed. "I want to enjoy myself all I can before Father sends me away to school."

Good-looking, vivacious, and unabashed, Vinnie had

more invitations and more callers. Emily, except for her beautiful hair and eyes, was plain, and, on first acquaintance, shy. How witty and charming she could be took their callers a little longer to discover.

Of them all, Benjamin Newton from Worcester interested Emily the most. A serious gentle person, penniless and in poor health, Ben was studying law in her father's office. As a Unitarian, he could tell her something of this liberal new religion.

"Seek the truth of religion in your own soul! Believe only what seems true to you. Man should be united by a spirit of brotherhood, not divided by nation, race, or creed."

How Father would disapprove of that, Emily thought —Father, Miss Lyon, and every minister she'd ever known.

With Ben, Emily could speak freely, and they had long conversations about life, death, and immortality. Through him she first heard of the courageous Lydia Maria Child, though Mrs. Child had been writing and lecturing against slavery and campaigning for women's rights since Emily was three years old. Around the same time William Lloyd Garrison had founded the anti-slavery paper *The Liberator*. Now, in the late 1840's, more and more people were listening to the fiery speeches of such abolitionists.

To Emily's father they were all dangerous fanatics, widening the breach between North and South.

Emily was especially interested in Mrs. Child's conviction that a woman should be something in herself and not a mere shadow of her husband, as Emily's mother was.

Emily wrote verses. So did Vinnie and other educated young girls. Like embroidering and piano playing, it was a ladylike accomplishment. But Emily was beginning to take her own verses more seriously. One day she made up her mind to show a few of them to Ben.

"These are good!" Ben's usually grave face lighted up. "You must keep working, Emily. Some day you may be a poet."

A poet! Emily knew better than to think he was merely being kind. Ben Newton never said anything he didn't mean.

So her verses were more than pretty combinations of words. They were poems—well not yet. That evening she read them again, already dissatisfied herself.

Sometimes the patterns of words had to be worked at. Sometimes they seemed to arrange themselves. If a verse felt right, it gave her the deepest satisfaction she had ever known.

During the two years Ben Newton was in Amherst he went on introducing her to new books, helped shape some of her ideas, and encouraged her to continue writing.

"I have taken him so for granted," she said when Ben moved to Worcester to practice law. "Now I don't know what I shall do."

Ben had not been gone long when she began writing to him and sending him poems. Once Ben sent her in return a book of Ralph Waldo Emerson's poems, with which she was deeply impressed. Emerson insisted on every person's right to his own belief. "Trust thyself," was one of his maxims. He wrote essays as well as poetry, and expressed a new kind of thought that had sprung up around Boston, called *Transcendentalism.*

Each human being was part of a supreme mind or "over-soul." Each must look for the truth of religion in his own soul, and not in an outside authority such as a church.

For Emily this had deep appeal. She was also drawn to Emerson's idea that everything in the world, even a drop of dew or a grain of sand, is a tiny copy of the entire universe.

In Amherst, a hundred miles from Boston, ideas like Emerson's aroused distrust. It was the sort of thing that led preachers to hold religious revivals. Vinnie, away at school now in Ipswich, Massachusetts, had come under the spell of a revival there. Emily and Austin were both receiving fervent letters from her, urging them to dedicate their lives to God.

"Austin," Emily said one day, "do you believe there is really another life after one dies? They all say so, but I wonder if they really know."

Austin expressed some of the same doubts.

"It's highly improper to be talking so," their mother scolded, overhearing them.

Emily and Austin exchanged glances as she walked away. Mother never questioned the idea of immortality or of anything else.

Soon Austin would be out of college and leaving Amherst to teach school. There would be no one in the house Emily could talk to like this. Close as she felt to Vinnie, they were not very much alike.

"Be thankful that I'm going," Austin teased her. "You complain that Father and I are always sparring lately."

It was true. Father and Austin were so different, Emily thought. Austin, tall and handsome now with a strong face and a mane of auburn hair, was imaginative, and interested in art and music. With Father everything was what he called "real life." He wanted Austin to think the same way.

The February that Emily was twenty-one she sent a long comic valentine letter to a young bachelor named William Howland. Howland sent it off to the *Springfield Republican*, and it appeared in the paper with this note:

> "The hand that wrote the following amusing medley . . . is capable of writing very fine things."

Though Emily's name had not been printed, the word quickly spread that the writer was Edward Dickinson's talented older daughter.

Emily was growing away from her former friends, even from Abiah Root. Many of the girls she knew had married and were starting homes. "I am different," Emily admitted. "I so like to be a child."

The more poetry she wrote, the more her letters sounded like poems. In poems and letters alike she had begun to use dashes in place of syllables here and there. Like a rest in a piece of music, the dash represented a pause.

Her New England upbringing had taught her the value of thrift, and Emily seldom wasted words.

> *The pattern of the sun*
> *Can fit but him alone*
> *For sheen must have a Disk*
> *To be a sun—*

She had written her first poems in the sentimental literary language of the time. Now she was beginning to trust her own, using everyday images of kitchen, barn, and field. All her life she had sung and listened to church hymns, and she took her rhythms and meters from these.

> *How still the Bells in Steeples stand*
> *Till swollen with the Sky*
> *They leap upon their silver Feet*
> *In frantic Melody!*

In a recent letter Ben Newton had repeated his prediction that she would someday become a real poet. But how much her writing was absorbing her no one in the family guessed. A light under Emily's door at night meant that she was probably reading.

The more time she spent alone writing, the less she liked leaving home on visits or attending social functions such as the annual Dickinson tea during Amherst College Commencement Week. To her father, the college treasurer, it was the social event of the year. As his daughter she had no choice but to attend, passing shyly among the guests, relieved when the last one had driven off.

Why was it that she felt so safe and serene alone, but so endangered by groups of people? As she expressed it once in a poem:

> *We introduce ourselves*
> *To Planets and to Flowers*
> *But with ourselves*
> *Have etiquettes*
> *Embarrassments*
> *And awes*

In December 1852 a bonfire in Amherst celebrated the election of Edward Dickinson to Congress.

"I'm so proud of you, Edward," Mrs. Dickinson said with tears in her eyes, "but you will be so far away—Washington!"

Emily was proud of her father, too, but she had a half-guilty sense of relief. Just a few days ago he had rebuked her like a child for wasting time on *Uncle Tom's Cabin*, the new novel by Mrs. Harriet Beecher Stowe.

Between sessions of Congress and for important occasions, Edward Dickinson came home, once for the opening of the first railroad in Amherst. Father was "Chief Marshal of the day," as Emily said. She herself watched the dedication ceremony from a wooded hill, alone. Ten years later she wrote the poem that begins:

> *I like to see it lap the Miles—*
> *And lick the Valleys up—*

Ben Newton had married meanwhile, but Emily went on sending him poems. Then one March day when Vinnie brought the *Springfield Daily Republican* home from the post office, there in the death column was Ben's name.

"Oh!" Emily gasped. As her mother and Vinnie came running, she pointed at it.

"And so young," Mother murmured, "but not as young as dear little Emily." For Emily Norcross had died only the year before.

Seizing a pen, Emily wrote on the sealed envelope flap of a letter to Austin: "Oh, Austin, Newton is dead. The first of my own friends."

When a popular Amherst Academy principal named Leonard Humphrey had died, she had felt the same deep sense of loss. "I was always in love with my teachers," she often said. To her, Ben had been a schoolmaster, as well as a kind of older brother. For some time after his death, Emily found it almost impossible to write.

Mrs. Dickinson eyed her anxiously. Poor spirits meant poor health. When Edward Dickinson summoned the family to Washington for a visit, she hoped that Emily would benefit by the change.

Emily helped Vinnie trim a new bonnet for the expedition, but up until the last minute, insisted that she was not going along herself. "Oh, do come, Emily," Vinnie said. "We'll see all the sights in Washington."

In the end Emily went along, but the round of state dinners and receptions at the nation's capital seemed ridiculous to her. "Such grandeur as you never saw," she wrote mockingly to friends. But on the way home she and

Vinnie stopped to visit a former schoolmate in Philadelphia. There, at the Arch Street Presbyterian Church, Emily found her next "teacher."

A famous pulpit orator, the Reverend Charles Wadsworth spoke simply but with tremendous fervor. He impressed Emily more than any minister she had ever heard. Something about him made her feel that he had suffered intensely. Yet he spoke with a resounding joy.

As his deep tones echoed through the church, she sat enthralled. In fascination she watched the changing expressions on his strong, rather plain face. As orthodox as any Amherst minister, he had the rare ability, as Emily said, of "scalping your naked soul."

Surely a man like this could explain to her the strange gap between her own innermost feelings and the teachings of the church. She went home determined to write to him.

6 · *I Started Early—Took My Dog—*

THERE WERE cobwebs in the corners of Austin's large square deserted room, and all the furniture had a layer of dust. Emily found the book she was looking for and fled.

Why did people have to grow up and go away, or grow up at all? she wondered. Everything was so much better when they were children.

Austin had given up teaching and was at Harvard University, studying law. Every time the subject came up there was a satisfied gleam in Father's eye. It was what he had wanted for Austin all along.

Father approved of Austin's friend Sue Gilbert, too. For a while Austin had been more interested in Sue's timid sister Mattie. Lately Sue seemed to be the one.

"You are so fortunate, Emily," Sue said to her one day. "Your whole family is living and still all together—or will be, I presume, when Austin returns." She watched the expression on Emily's face. "What fine times we had when he was here!"

"And will again when he comes back," Emily said. In

her next letter to Austin she was careful to mention how much Sue Gilbert missed him.

A striking dark-haired girl, Sue was the daughter of a tavern keeper, the youngest of seven children. An orphan at eleven, she had lived with various relatives for more than half of her life. Having to fend for herself had given her a self possession that Emily admired. Witty and vivacious, Sue was as much at ease with a parlorful of people as she was alone with Emily. And she was not at all in awe of Father. Sue read a great deal, including the latest books and magazines, and had more feeling for poetry than anyone Emily knew. She could not imagine any girl she would rather have as a sister-in-law.

The year in Cambridge had given Austin a citified air that made Emily uneasy lately. She remembered his hints of settling in Chicago or one of the other growing cities in the West.

Emily was not the only one against it. "Amherst is where you belong," their father said, when Austin came home. "I want you to come in with me as a law partner."

When Austin finally agreed, the whole family was overjoyed. This was the way things should be. And on July 1, 1856, he and Sue Gilbert were married.

After fifteen years on Pleasant Street, the Dickinsons were now back in the family homestead. Squire Dickinson had bought it, and was building Austin a large frame house next door.

Any change in her surroundings, even this one, disturbed Emily. But now she had more of the privacy she loved. The huge brick house, screened by thick hemlock hedges from passers-by, was surrounded by lawns, shrubbery, and large shade trees where birds sang. Across the road was a sweep of meadowland.

From her room at the southwest corner of the house, Emily saw breathtaking sunsets, and later wrote stanzas such as this:

> *This—is the land—the Sunset washes—*
> *These—are the Banks of the Yellow Sea—*
> *Where it rose—or whither it rushes—*
> *These—are the Western Mystery!*

In no time at all a path was worn from the back door of the homestead to the Evergreens, as Sue called her house.

"I wish I could look on her as you do, Emily," Vinnie sometimes said. From the first, she and their new sister-in-law often clashed. Emily welcomed Sue into the family with affectionate notes and verses.

Emily was twenty-five, and Vinnie twenty-three. "Well, your son has married and settled down," people were beginning to remark to Mrs. Dickinson. "Now what about your two daughters?"

"That will depend upon their father," Mrs. Dickinson replied with dignity. "Mr. Dickinson is very particular."

Not too particular to let his son marry the daughter of a drunken tavern keeper, people noticed. It was whispered that the Squire's stern attitude toward his daughters' suitors frightened some of them away.

At a time when all sewing was done by hand, and even butter was made at home, there was more than enough for the sisters to do. "I don't know how I should get along without you," their mother often said.

Vinnie liked to wield a mop, broom, or rug beater. She did a great deal of the daily house cleaning and the heavy cleaning in spring and fall.

"Spring cleaning is pestilence," Emily said. She preferred what she called the butterfly part of the housekeeping, baking cookies or concocting puddings.

There was a reading club in the village and lectures at the lyceum. Young people gathered in the parlors of Amherst for singing, piano playing, and charades. In summer they took excursions to the summit of Mount Holyoke, or picnicked in the Pelham Hills. In winter there were sleigh rides, fudge parties, and when the sap began to run in the maples, sugaring off parties.

In all of this Vinnie took an active part, and when Emily felt like it, she went along. More often than not now, she stayed away. Her frail health gave her an excuse for frequently avoiding church. In one of her poems she wrote:

> *Some keep the Sabbath going to Church—*
> *I keep it, staying at Home—*
> *With a Bobolink for a Chorister—*
> *And an Orchard, for a Dome—*
>
> (first stanza)

There were times when she would run upstairs at the sound of the doorbell. If her parents had guests, as they often did, Emily might appear in the parlor for only a moment or not even appear at all. Such rudeness was difficult to explain away.

Emily could not explain it even to herself. She knew only that the sound of the doorbell set up a feeling of panic. To her sister and brother and to close friends she spoke of it sometimes, in half-sad, half-mocking tones.

In the poem below, written when she was in her twenties, she may have been expressing her feeling about it.

> *I never hear the word "escape"*
> *Without a quicker blood,*
> *A sudden expectation,*
> *A flying attitude!*
>
> *I never hear of prisons broad*
> *By soldiers battered down,*
> *But I tug childish at my bars*
> *Only to fail again!*

Then there were those long solitary walks that Emily took. They were not proper or even safe. "You must have a dog to accompany you," her father said.

Carlo, the large shaggy brown dog he bought her, was named after a character in a book she had just read. Where Emily went, Carlo went—through tall meadow grass or crackling underbrush, to the top of some lonely hill. After dark, if she went no farther than Austin's and Sue's house, a lantern in her hand, Carlo trudged along. Perhaps he found his way into one of her poems.

I started Early—Took my Dog—
And visited the Sea—
The Mermaids in the Basement
Came out to look at me—

(first stanza)

Carlo was the kind of companion Emily liked. "You know what I think, but you don't tell," she said, looking into his understanding brown eyes.

People, on the other hand, were so willing to expose their souls—before a whole churchful of others at times.

Emily was the only member of the family who had not officially joined the church. Sue tried to persuade her and sometimes they quarreled about it. Emily still could not honestly accept some of the doctrines of the church.

To Charles Wadsworth, the preacher she had heard in Philadelphia, she had been pouring out some of her doubts. A box hidden in her bureau drawer held a growing number of his replies.

Rereading one of his letters, Emily would hear again the Philadelphia minister's impassioned tones. Charles Wadsworth was in his forties, a married man, and miles away. She had seen him only once. Yet she already thought of him as her dearest friend. Perhaps some day he could call on her in Amherst. To a daughter of Edward Dickinson there was nothing unusual in this idea. Many a distinguished visitor traveled out of his way to knock at the Dickinsons' door.

Meanwhile the poems Emily considered good enough

to keep were growing in number. When she was satisfied with one she would copy it in ink. Then she would put it with a few others, sewing the papers together into little booklets. These she placed for safekeeping in the bottom of her cherry-wood bureau.

Most of the poems were filled with flowers and birds, sunset and snow, crickets and frost. But nature was just a means of expressing her feelings about all of life. An ant, a beetle, a stone were as worthy of poetry as anything else, as she showed in her poem *A Bird came down the Walk* and in *How happy is the little Stone*.

She wanted to say as much as possible in the fewest words and say it truthfully. And this she achieved more and more as time went on.

"The words 'I' or 'Me' in my verses refer to a supposed person," she told Sue, "not to myself."

Sue smiled. "Be that as it may, Emily, the last one you sent me, *To fight aloud, is very brave*, is superb. I read it aloud to Austin, and he agrees. You should be appearing in print. We *must* talk to Sam Bowles."

Samuel Bowles was the editor of the *Daily Springfield Republican* and a friend of Austin's.

Married to a woman who was uninterested in writing, Samuel Bowles enjoyed talking with Emily when he came to Amherst to visit Austin and Sue. Between visits he welcomed her startling letters. He praised her writing talent, and talked of publishing some of her poems. Aside from Dr. Josiah Holland, associate editor of the *Republican*, he was the first professional literary man she had ever known.

Though he was only a few years older than Emily, he was always "Mr. Bowles" or "Mr. Sam." A handsomely bearded man, with a hearty infectious laugh, he had warmth, humor, and intelligence. He made light of Emily's shyness, till sometimes it melted away.

Samuel Bowles introduced her to new authors, just as Ben Newton had. But Samuel Bowles had the pressure of editing a newspaper. He had a wife and children and many friends, and no time for a steady exchange of letters. Now and then Emily received a cheerful note from him but that was all.

A man of tremendous nervous energy, he was often overworked and Emily worried about his health, particularly if he was at any distance. "My friends are my 'estate,'" she said once, and Samuel Bowles had become an important part of her estate.

For six years she had been writing to Charles Wadsworth, treasuring his replies like sacred relics. The Philadelphia minister was continually in her thoughts.

Then one day in the early part of 1860 Charles Wadsworth himself knocked at the mansion door. He was visiting a friend in Northampton, less than ten miles away. Miss Dickinson lived so close by he had decided to call on her, he explained.

So here he was, one of her "masters," his deep voice reverberating through the house. In awe Emily looked into the piercing black eyes and watched the changing expressions cross his face.

On Mr. Wadsworth's hat was the black crepe that meant mourning. She had noticed it instantly.

"Someone has died?" she asked. Though Mr. Wadsworth never referred to his family in letters, Emily knew that he had a wife and several children.

"Yes," he explained, "my mother."

"Oh," Emily said softly.

7 · *The Soul Selects Her Own Society*

EMILY COULD bake a loaf of rye and Indian bread that brought a gleam of pleasure to her father's eye. He refused to eat bread baked by any other hand. She could darn a sock so skillfully that he couldn't say where the hole had been. He enjoyed having Emily cater to him, an excuse she gave for not leaving home.

One of her greatest pleasures was her flower garden, where wildflowers bloomed as well as roses, lilies, and jasmine. But for the deepest satisfaction she turned inward to the world of her imagination.

> *To make a prairie it takes a clover and one bee*
> *One clover, and a bee,*
> *And revery.*
> *The revery alone will do,*
> *If bees are few.*

The hours for writing were too few. Church services, club meetings, and gossiping neighbors took up time.

Emily preferred a few people she could feel really close to, though even these she seldom saw. A large part of any friendship was carried on by means of notes, sent sometimes with a jar of jelly, some choice apples, or a flower. "The Soul selects her own Society—" she wrote in one of her poems, "Then—shuts the Door—"

The family had come to accept Emily's ways, but Austin and her father became annoyed at times when she refused to see a family friend.

Vinnie indulged Emily in her ways, willingly answering the doorbell, or delivering notes and flowers for her. With a flash of her dark eyes she quickly disposed of prying questions. "Why didn't Emily go to the sewing circle like everybody else?" "Why should she?" was Vinnie's retort. "If she's more contented to stay at home?"

Austin's marriage was not turning out as the family had hoped. His beautiful Sue was more self-centered than any of them had guessed. Being the wife of young Squire Dickinson seemed more important to her than Austin himself. The Dickinsons in the brick house next door shook their heads over the amounts of money she spent. Sue was never happier than when the driveway of the Evergreens was crowded with the carriages of guests, and the whole house ablaze with lights.

"Glitter," Emily summed it up.

Sue could be cutting and often hurt Emily, but Emily usually forgave her and, in spite of everything, went on admiring her and sending her poems.

Sue and Austin had no son to carry on the family name, or any children at all as yet. Emily knew how this must prey upon Austin, and anything that troubled Austin troubled her.

Sometime in 1860, the year she was thirty years old, Emily fell in love, though who the man was no one has ever been sure. Some of the people who have studied her poems and letters think it was Charles Wadsworth, and others, Samuel Bowles. A man she called "Master" had begun appearing in letters and poems.

By now she had copied 150 poems into the little booklets. She had written about friendship, about life and death, about coming to know one's self. Now the poems were centering on love.

" 'Tis so much joy! 'Tis so much joy!" one of the poems begins, and another, "Come slowly, Eden!" There were also poems in which she saw herself dressed in white or used the word wife, as if she considered herself married in spirit.

Then, within the year, Emily found out that the man she loved did not love her.

From almost delirious joy she plunged into deepest despair. For months afterward, in handwriting as chaotic as her state of mind, she poured her emotions into her writing. Poems such as *I felt a Funeral, in my Brain* show how overwhelmed she felt, and in some of her letters there are hints that she even feared losing her mind. No poem or letter was dated, but handwriting experts have guessed at the dates by a study of the changing script.

More and more of her words began with capital letters, and more were underlined. She used dashes more freely than ever, giving a breathless effect.

One poem written during the crisis struck a different, more optimistic note:

> *"Hope" is the thing with feathers—*
> *That perches in the soul—*
> *And sings the tune without the words—*
> *And never stops—at all—*
>
> (first stanza)

The Republican Abraham Lincoln had been elected President on a platform calling for the end of slavery in the United States territories. He took office as the Confederates fired on the Union ship *Star of the West* at Fort Sumter, South Carolina. The Civil War had begun.

Southern students at Amherst College left in a body. Northern students and young men of the town rushed to enlist in the Union army. Soon there were Amherst people receiving reports of their sons' deaths.

The war reached Emily obliquely. No one in her family fought. For months she had suffered from a strange sense of terror. Her writing gave her something solid to lean on.

In May 1861, one of her poems appeared, unsigned, in the *Springfield Republican*. It begins like this:

> *I taste a liquor never brewed—*
> *From Tankards scooped in Pearl—*

In June a son, Edward Dickinson, was born to Austin and Sue, a frail, sickly child who kept his mother preoccupied. Sue had little time to think of poetry these days. She and Emily had drawn somewhat apart. Yet Emily went on sending her poems. Two years before she had written a poem that is now famous: *Safe in their Alabaster Chambers*. The second stanza was not to Sue's liking, and Emily had written a new one. When Sue told her it didn't go with the ghostly shimmer of the first stanza, Emily wrote another. "Is this frostier?" she asked. Sue could tell her, she hinted, if only she would be sincere. Then she admitted that her greatest ambition was to, some day, make Sue and Austin proud of her.

Austin seemed out of sorts. The birth of a son had done nothing to bring him any closer to his wife. Mother was complaining of neuralgia, and Father was irritable. "Such a family!" Vinnie said. "I really despair of you all." She herself had taken to adopting cats. Emily had always looked forward to March, but this year she hardly noticed.

One blustery day Vinnie was out at the clotheslines energetically beating rugs, long past the time she usually went to the post office for the mail. Now she came into the house, her cheeks rosy, bringing with her a rush of tingling air.

"Can't you go now?" Emily begged, hoping desperately for letters from the few friends who were so important to her.

There were no letters that day, but in the Original Poetry column in the *Springfield Republican* was her poem *Safe in their Alabaster Chambers*. In bitter disappointment she stared at the lines she had written and rewritten so many times. The editors had changed some of the words. It was no longer her poem. She was glad she had not signed her name.

On his doctor's advice, Samuel Bowles, who had developed heart trouble, was going to Europe, a whole ocean away. Charles Wadsworth, meanwhile, had been called to a church in San Francisco, a whole continent away.

Emily felt abandoned. More desperately than ever she turned to her poetry. At times she knew with deep certainty that it was good. With this came the feeling that life was good, too.

At other times doubt crept in. Who said that her work was good? She herself, a few friends, a few editors. Editors distorted her verses for the sake of mere rhyme. Friends sometimes hinted that her poems, while remarkable, were strange "airy" things, not rooted enough in earth.

Perhaps she was no poet at all. Dark overwhelming forces seemed to rush toward her at the thought.

As if in answer, the *Atlantic Monthly* for April 1862 ran the article "Letter to a Young Contributor." The author was Thomas Wentworth Higginson, whose books Emily knew and liked. In his article, he wrote as if directly to her. He urged young writers to charge their style with life, and to work and rework. No word that could be done without should be left in. One word could express volumes, and half a sentence a whole lifetime. "Literature is attar of roses," he wrote. "One distilled drop from a million blossoms."

Higginson spoke of the mystery and majesty of words

and the importance of the poet's calling. In the flowery language of the time, he said what Emily herself believed.

She read on to the end, then went back to reread the words, "charge your style with life."

Surely the man who had written this could tell her what she wanted to know about her own writing. Emily sat down at the first opportunity with pen and notepaper.

8 · Barefoot Rank

A FEW DAYS later in Worcester, Massachusetts, Thomas Wentworth Higginson opened Emily's letter.

"Mr. Higginson," he read, "are you too deeply occupied to say if my verse is alive?" She was not sure herself, she explained, and had no one to ask. At the end she urged him to keep the whole thing a secret. There was no signature on the letter. As if hiding from view, Emily had written her name on a card, tucked into a smaller envelope.

With her letter were four poems, without titles, like all her others. *Safe in their Alabaster Chambers* was one. Another was a poem which, today, is a great favorite. It begins:

> *I'll tell you how the Sun rose—*
> *A Ribbon at a time—*

In his "Letter to a Young Contributor," Mr. Higginson had urged that dashes be used very sparingly. This young contributor had filled her poems with dashes. Many of the nouns began with capital letters—a style no longer in fashion. Worse still, the young lady seemed to know nothing of rhyme or even grammar and spelling. There were flashes of something new and original in her verses, but in his opinion she had a long way to go if she ever hoped to become a poet.

Thomas Wentworth Higginson was a Unitarian minister who had left the pulpit to write and lecture on such subjects as the abolition of slavery and women's rights. As an ex-minister, he was used to having people lean on him. He would do what he could to help poor Miss Dickinson.

Emily read Mr. Higginson's reply with a mixture of excitement and disappointment. Though he praised the originality of her poems, it was clear that he didn't know what to make of them.

One of the poems was *We play at Paste—till qualified for Pearl.* By including it, Emily hinted that she was no longer a beginner, but a poet, eager to perfect her art. Mr. Higginson, it was clear, thought otherwise. He urged her to master grammar, improve her rhyme, and try for smoother, more flowing lines.

Emily read the letter again. At least Mr. Higginson took her seriously. And she warmed to the kindness and sympathy between the lines.

Ten days later she sent off another note and three more poems.

Mr. Higginson had asked her age, and she answered by

saying, "I made no verse but one or two until—this winter—sir—"

Then she confessed, "I had a terror—since September
—I could tell to none—and so I sing, as the Boy does by
the Burying Ground—because I am afraid—"

She answered the questions about her favorite books
and about her friends. Ben Newton was the friend who
had taught her Immortality. "But venturing too close
himself, he never returned," she said.

Samuel Bowles, the other friend she mentioned, "was
not content I should be his scholar—so he left the land."

Her companions? "Hills—sir—and the Sundown—
and a Dog—as large as myself that my Father bought me
—They are better than Beings—because they know—but
do not tell—"

"I have a brother and sister—my mother does not care
for thought—and a father, too busy with his briefs—to
notice what we do—"

She was thirty-one years old, but spoke of herself, her
brother, and sister as children.

She begged her new teacher to tell her how to become a
poet. In the same sentence she suggested that perhaps, like
melody or witchcraft, it could not be taught.

Among the poems enclosed with this second letter was
one meant to be sent to a friend, with a flower:

> *South Winds jostle them—*
> *Bumblebees come—*
> *Hover—hesitate—*
> *Drink, and are gone—*

Butterflies pause
On their passage Cashmere—
I—softly plucking,
Present them here!

Another was a beautiful poem with the following first stanza:

Of all the Sounds despatched abroad,
There's not a Charge to me
Like that old measure in the Boughs—
That phraseless Melody—
The Wind does—working like a Hand,
Whose fingers Comb the Sky—
Then quiver down—with tufts of Tune—
Permitted Gods, and me—

The third was a love poem of seven stanzas, the first of which appears below:

There came a Day at Summer's full,
Entirely for me—
I thought that such were for the Saints,
Where Resurrections—be—

This time, feeling bolder, Emily signed the letter, "Your friend, E. Dickinson."

The three poems brought more praise than the first set, as well as further criticism.

"I have had few pleasures as deep as your opinion,"

Emily wrote back, and in the same letter, "My dying Tutor told me that he would like to live till I had been a poet . . ."

Since she seemed to have trouble rhyming properly, Mr. Higginson had said, perhaps she should drop rhyme altogether. But Emily explained that she "could not drop the Bells whose jingling cooled my Tramp."

In most poetry of the time, lines ended in exact rhymes. Many of Emily's poems were rhymed in this way. But when it suited her purpose, she used other, more subtle kinds. One of these was *suspended rhyme*, in which different vowel sounds are followed by the same consonant:

> human
>
> common

Another was *imperfect rhyme*. Here, two rhyming words end with the same vowel sound, followed by different consonants:

> field
>
> steal

Mr. Higginson had advised Emily to be in no hurry to publish her poems. This made her smile. Nothing was further from her mind, she assured him. "If fame belonged to me, I could not escape her—if she did not, the longest day would pass me on the chase . . . My Barefoot—Rank is better—"

In her heart Emily knew that Thomas Higginson would never be the critic and teacher she had hoped for.

But she was grateful for any comment from the man who had written as he had in the *Atlantic Monthly* about the importance of the poet's calling.

Her solitary life dismayed him, and he urged her to mingle more. Emily wrote back, shyly asking if he would have time to be the friend he felt she needed.

More curious than ever, Mr. Higginson asked her to send a picture of herself.

Instead, there came this description: "I had no portrait now, but I am small, like the Wren, and my Hair is bold, like the Chestnut Bur—and my eyes like the sherry the guest leaves in the glass."

In August Mr. Higginson's letters stopped coming. Autumn arrived. Apples ripened in the orchard, Concord grapes hung in heavy blue clusters, and the walnuts and hazelnuts were brown.

With her dog at her side, Emily walked through the crackling leaves, filling her basket. It soothed her and cleared her mind. "But why don't I have a letter from Mr. Higginson?" she said to Carlo. "Have I displeased him?" That evening she wrote and asked.

Thomas Higginson had been drilling a company of Massachusetts soldiers. In November he took over leadership of the first official regiment of ex-slaves in the Union army. Occupied as he was, Thomas Higginson, now a colonel, took time to write to her from an army camp.

At last the war was touching Emily more directly. Fearful that she might lose her new friend, she wrote back, "I should have liked to see you before you became improbable."

Samuel Bowles had returned from Europe, and Emily wrote to him at once. As she had so many times before, she told him how much she thought of him. And she begged him not to start working again until he was really well.

Only a few days later, he came to Amherst, and the Dickinsons were delighted. Samuel Bowles was a favorite with all of them.

"Come down, Emily. Sam's here," Austin called from the foot of the stairs.

There was no answer. At the sound of Samuel Bowles's deep-throated laugh, Emily was too overcome with emotion. When Vinnie came looking for her, she gave her a little note for him.

This, after the devotion-filled letters Emily had been writing! Samuel Bowles felt snubbed but, in his light-hearted way, he made a joke of it, sending his regards to the "Queen Recluse" in a letter to Austin. In another he sent Emily a message, chiding her for ignoring him.

Emily meanwhile had given up colored dresses, wearing only white, a symbol, apparently, that she was dedicating her life to someone or something.

9 · I'm Nobody! Who Are You?

PEOPLE found her poetry puzzling. Editors and critics like Samuel Bowles, Dr. Holland, and Thomas Higginson thought most of it unsuitable to print. Emily was becoming resigned to this.

Far from being discouraged, she was writing one poem after another. In 1862 alone, she wrote 365, among them the one beginning:

> *This is my letter to the World*
> *That never wrote to Me—*

If her poems were published at all, she would remain anonymous. There would be no froglike croaking of her own name.

> *I'm nobody! Who are you?*
> *Are you—Nobody—too?*
> *Then there's a pair of us?*
> *Don't tell! They'd advertise—you know!*

How dreary—to be—Somebody!
How public—like a Frog—
To tell one's name—the livelong June—
To an admiring Bog!

During 1863, still distraught, Emily went on writing. That year there were about 140 poems she considered good enough to join the others tucked away in her bottom bureau drawer.

Though she knew now that Thomas Higginson could teach her little, she went on pretending to be his student. About a year before, she had complained in one of her poems of being "shut up in prose" just as she had been shut in a closet, as a child—to keep her still.

Here was another who wanted to shut Emily up in prose. Nevertheless, she considered Thomas Higginson her friend.

Most of Emily's letters that year went to her cousins, Louisa and Fanny Norcross in Boston, who had just lost their father. Louisa was now twenty-one and Fanny sixteen, but Emily continued to speak as if she and they were small children.

"Fanny and Loo are such geese," Vinnie said, and no one else gave them credit for great intelligence. But Emily had taken them to her heart, and loved them as they were. With them she shared some of her troubles as well as details of her daily life omitted from letters to others.

In February and again in April she went to Boston to see an eye doctor, staying with her cousins. They were kind to her, but she found being away from home more painful than the eye ailment. She would be willing to *walk* to Amherst, she wrote to Vinnie, sleeping in the bushes along the way.

One January day in 1866 when Amherst was buried in snow, Carlo died. Emily was heartbroken. She had lost her "shaggy ally," as she called him. No other dog could ever replace him.

About a month afterward, Emily opened the *Springfield Republican* to find a poem about a snake she had written the year before. It began:

A narrow Fellow in the Grass
Occasionally rides—

The meaning of the third and fourth lines had been altered by a change in her punctuation. Editors!

And who had given them the poem? Sue, of course. For years now Sue had been ambitious for her protégée. "We must launch you," she often said.

Emily was hurt and angry. What would Thomas Higginson think of this? She had told him that she did not "print." Now she would have to apologize. Not to publish had become a point of honor with her.

For the next few years Emily went on writing but more slowly. Her letters to Thomas Higginson were fewer. When she did write, he was slow in answering.

"Sometimes I take out your letters & verses," he explained once, "and when I feel their strange power, it is not strange that I find it hard to write & that long months pass. I have the greatest desire to see you, always feeling that perhaps if I could once take you by the hand I might be something to you; but till then you only enshroud yourself in this fiery mist & I cannot reach you, but only rejoice in the rare sparkles of light.

"It is hard for me to understand how you can live so alone, with thoughts of such a quality coming up in you & even the companionship of your dog withdrawn."

Then he asked her if she ever came to Boston. "All ladies do," he said, inviting her to a meeting of the Women's Club at which he would read a paper on the Greek goddesses.

Politely but firmly Emily refused. Her eye doctor did want her to return to Boston for a checkup, she admitted, but leaving home was impossible. Her father was too accustomed to having her nearby.

She urged Colonel Higginson to come to Amherst instead, explaining, "I do not cross my father's ground to any house or town."

10 · *I Know That Is Poetry*

ONE AUGUST day in 1870 Thomas Wentworth Higginson mounted the stone steps of the Dickinsons' house.

Maggie Maher, who was now their maid, led him into the front parlor, and took his calling card upstairs.

For eight years Emily had been hoping for his visit. Now that he was here, she had to summon all her courage to go and greet him.

In the parlor below, Colonel Higginson looked curiously around him. The draperies were drawn, closing out the August sun. The air was filled with the fragrance of flowers, and now he noticed bouquets everywhere. The dark heavy furniture was stiffly arranged. The whole house was utterly quiet.

Finally he heard soft pattering footsteps, like those of a child. Then into the room glided a plain little woman with a nunlike air. Her white dress and blue shawl, like the furnishings of the parlor, struck him as oddly out-of-date. But like everyone else, Thomas Higginson was drawn to Emily's large, wondering, rather frightened eyes.

She put two orange day lilies into his hand, saying,

"These are my introduction." Then in a low breathless tone—"Forgive me if I am frightened; I never see strangers and hardly know what I say." After a little pause she began to talk, stopping now and then to urge him to talk instead, but going on herself.

Occasionally Colonel Higginson put in a question. And as Emily described her early life, her father loomed large. "There is his picture. I was always in awe of him," she confessed.

Thomas Higginson glanced at the man in the framed photograph on the table and was not surprised.

Urged on, Emily poured out her thoughts.

"Truth is such a rare thing, it is delightful to tell it," she said. When Colonel Higginson gently hinted that her life must be lonely and not much fun, she declared, "I find ecstacy in living—the mere sense of living is joy enough."

"Hmm." With a puzzled frown, Colonel Higginson looked into her eyes. "But you say you never leave the grounds, and see few visitors. Don't you sometimes suffer for want of something to do?"

"I never thought of conceiving that I could ever have the slightest approach to such a want in all future time," Emily promptly replied. After a little pause she added, "I feel that I have not expressed myself strongly enough."

So complete was her withdrawal by now that she avoided even the dressmaker. Vinnie, who was the same size, took her place for the fitting of the white dresses she always wore.

Emily mixed details of her daily life with statements

that startled and puzzled Colonel Higginson as much as her letters had.

"If I read a book and it makes my whole body so cold no fire can ever warm me, I know *that* is poetry," she said. "If I feel physically as if the top of my head were taken off, I know *that* is poetry. These are the only ways I know. Is there any other way?"

Thomas Higginson's description of Emily is one of the few there are. Three years later he paid another visit to the brick house behind the tall hemlock hedges but, apparently, made no extensive notes.

In the same year, 1873, Edward Dickinson was re-elected to the Massachusetts Legislature. Seventy years old now, his work in Boston was beginning to affect his health.

Emily was forty-three. She was still writing, but turning out fewer poems than in her early thirties.

To the people of Amherst she had become almost a myth. Boys who delivered goods to the back door told of seeing her white-clad fleeing figure. Children peeked through the Dickinson hedges, hoping for a glimpse of her. She no longer went as far as her brother Austin's house next door. And she would not expose even her handwriting to the public gaze. When she wrote a letter, her sister Lavinia addressed the envelope. She had turned her back on the world, it was rumored, because of a disappointment in love.

Even to the few people she saw, her life seemed monotonous and uneventful. To Emily it was rich and satisfying. She had withdrawn to her father's house and grounds, but, in a deeper sense, she had not withdrawn from the world at all. From the store of her own memories, from her reading, and from her imaginative sympathy with the lives of those she loved, she was probing the mysteries of love, death, and immortality. Among the poems she had written and tucked away during the past ten years was the famous *Because I could not stop for Death*.

Many of her poems shaped themselves in her mind as she went about her household duties. These she would jot down on the margin of a newspaper, on the back of an envelope, or on a scrap of brown grocery paper.

She liked having her poems read by those who responded to them, even if only in part. A few relatives and friends—this was her audience as well as her "estate."

American industry was growing. Cities were expanding. Railroads were being built. There were thousands of new mechanical inventions. But the vigor that was building the nation had no counterpart in the literature of the day. Poetry in particular lacked the breath of life.

Literary men were beginning to cry out for a stronger, more honest kind of verse. The year of his first visit to Emily, Thomas Higginson wrote an article on the subject for the *Atlantic Monthly*. Poets and novelists, especially the Americans, were not probing deeply into human emotion, he complained. Not even Ralph Waldo Emerson or Nathaniel Hawthorne had plumbed the depths. The American poet of passion was yet to come.

Lying in his desk as he wrote the words were a number of Emily Dickinson's poems.

II · *Success Is Counted Sweetest*

ONE JUNE evening in 1874 as Mrs. Dickinson, Emily, and Vinnie were at supper, Austin burst in, with a telegram in his hand.

"Father is very sick. You and I must go to him in Boston, Vinnie, and the last train has left." No one thought of suggesting that Emily go. Before the horse was even harnessed, another message arrived from Boston. Edward Dickinson, stricken while speaking before the Massachusetts Legislature, was dead.

"Dead!" Emily said over and over to herself. "Father dead!" She thought of his last afternoon at home. Vinnie had taken a nap, and Emily had suggested an errand that took her mother out of the house. For some unexplained reason she wanted to be alone with her father. They sat in the back parlor, reading and talking a little. Squire Dickinson was pleased. Shyly he said, "I'd like this afternoon not to end."

Emily had been flustered. She knew in her heart how much she meant to her father but was unused to his showing it like this.

"There, Father," Austin said before the funeral, kissing his dead father's face, "I never dared do that while you were alive."

During the funeral Emily stayed upstairs. The only friend she could bear to see was Samuel Bowles.

All her married life Mrs. Dickinson's world had revolved around her husband's, and just a year after his death, she suffered a stroke.

Emily cooked special dishes for her mother, soothed her when her spirits were low, and assured her that she was getting better. She pitied her for having to lie helpless, a person with so little to occupy her mind. Gradually her mother came to seem like the child, and she the mother.

Caring for an invalid left little time for anything else— "a few moments at night for books, after the rest sleep," Emily confided to Thomas Higginson. When he asked if there was any time at all for poetry, she told him it was her only "playmate."

> *To see the Summer Sky*
> *Is Poetry, though never in a Book it lie—*
> *True Poems flee—*

Emily had long given up any thought of having more of her work published. But now a woman named Helen Hunt Jackson came to Amherst. Under the pen name H.H., Mrs. Jackson had written the novel *Ramona*, several other novels, and a book of verse. One of the most popular women authors in America, she was a friend of

Thomas Wentworth Higginson. She had seen Emily's unusual poems, and was enthusiastic about them.

Her own publisher was planning a new series of books to be published anonymously. One volume would be made up of poems written by famous poets but never before published. Readers would be asked to guess who had written each. Mrs. Jackson wanted to include a poem by Emily Dickinson.

"No, indeed," Emily said. "I couldn't think of it."

"You say you find pleasure in reading my verses," Mrs. Jackson chided her. "Why not let others have the same pleasure in reading yours?"

Emily liked Helen Hunt Jackson, a warm, charming woman and the only literary person who had ever given her poetry wholehearted praise. In distress, she begged Colonel Higginson to let her say that he opposed it.

Without pressing Emily further, Mrs. Jackson submitted to her publisher Emily's poem *Success is counted sweetest.*

Meanwhile, Emily was writing to Samuel Bowles several times a month. Her father, since his death, was in her thoughts a great deal, so sometimes she spoke of him, sometimes of Bowles himself. She begged him to be careful of his health but there was none of the fear and desperation of her earlier letters. However, she still thought of him as godlike, telling him that he had "the most triumphant Face out of Paradise."

In the summer of 1877 Bowles came to the mansion one day when there were other visitors. Emily refused to join them, but Samuel Bowles stood at the foot of the stairs.

"Emily, you damned rascal!" he shouted. "Stop this nonsense! I've traveled a long way to see you. Now come down here."

Emily was delighted and came down at once, staying as long as Bowles was there. That evening she wrote him a note signed "Your Rascal," adding that she had "washed the Adjective."

Soon afterward Samuel Bowles became seriously ill, and the next January he died.

For Emily it was the second great loss in four years, but less of a shock than the sudden death of her father. For twenty years she had been fearing and expecting it. She was soon trying to comfort Mr. Bowles's widow, Mary, and some of his closest friends.

While her father lived, Judge Otis Lord of Salem, an old friend, had paid a visit to Amherst every year. Now, even though Edward Dickinson was gone, he and his wife continued the visits.

Then, on Emily's forty-seventh birthday, Mrs. Lord died. Otis Lord himself was sixty-eight years old. A lonely widower now, he welcomed Emily's sympathy. And Emily welcomed the visits of her father's friend. Before long she and Judge Lord discovered that they loved each other.

From then on Emily wore a ring that Otis Lord gave her. She went on writing poetry. She went on wearing white. She still refused to see most people face to face. But her letters to Judge Lord show how much happiness his love brought her.

Not everyone rejoiced with her. Otis Lord's two

nieces, who hoped to inherit his money, were bitterly resentful. Sue Dickinson, who wanted Emily nearby to support her in family quarrels, spoke scornfully of the conservative judge, "a perfect figurehead for the Supreme Court."

Relations had been strained for some time. Unloved by his wife, Austin was like a stranger in his own home. Vinnie no longer even spoke to Sue. And Emily found it more and more difficult to forgive her sister-in-law's spiteful ways. The strongest bond between the two households was Gilbert, Austin's second son and third child, the delight of his parents and aunts alike.

In October 1878, Helen Hunt Jackson and her husband visited Emily again. The book of unsigned verses by noted American poets was going to press. "Please," Mrs. Jackson begged, "let us include your verse *Success.*" Again Emily steadfastly refused. Within a few days she received a desperate letter. "Can you refuse the only thing I may ever ask of you?" Mrs. Jackson pleaded.

Emily gave in, and her poem appeared in a collection containing poems by John Greenleaf Whittier, Ralph Waldo Emerson, Louisa May Alcott, Helen Hunt Jackson, and others.

> *Success is counted sweetest*
> *By those who ne'er succeed.*

So began the poem she had written twenty years before. In its twelve short lines five changes had been made. Reviewers of the book thought Emerson had written the poem.

"Ralph Waldo Emerson!" Vinnie exclaimed. "Oh, Emily! I'm so proud of you."

"But it doesn't say what I *meant!*" Emily cried out. "They've altered it." She was glad her name had not appeared. She continued her friendship with Helen Hunt Jackson but never again discussed publication.

Anything written by a friend she read eagerly, generous with praise. For herself publication was too public. "How can you print a piece of your own soul?" she asked Mrs. Jackson once. For her own satisfaction alone, she wrote on.

When Judge Lord seemed to be urging marriage, she gently turned it aside. She was needed at home to nurse her mother, she said.

One summer evening she was working in her garden. The sun had just dropped behind the Pelham hills. A fresh dampness rose from the earth around the roots of the lilies and heliotropes. Her mother had gone to sleep at last. She would have a few moments to herself.

Though no one was expected, she heard the ring of the doorbell. A moment later Vinnie came hurrying across the grass. "The gentleman with the deep voice wants to see you, Emily!" It was Charles Wadsworth.

"How long did it take you to get here?" Emily asked.

"Twenty years," Mr. Wadsworth replied with a smile.

Emily still regarded him with the awe of a young girl. For many years now his portrait had hung on the wall of her room, one of her "masters."

This was the last time she ever saw him, for two years

later Charles Wadsworth died. She called him her "dearest earthly friend" but actually knew very little about him. Now she wrote to his friends, asking about his children and whether he had brothers and sisters. But what she wanted most was to be assured that he lived on in some other sphere. The question of immortality still haunted her.

12 · *The Poets Light But Lamps*

TO EMILY each love or friendship was separate, and individual.

A few weeks after Charles Wadsworth's death, she sat down at her desk to write a loving letter to Otis Lord. In it she spoke of Wadsworth as her "Philadelphia." She wrote a few lines more, when Vinnie came bursting in.

"Emily," she asked, "did you see anything in the paper today—anything concerning us?"

"Why no, Vinnie, what?" Emily asked, alarmed by her sister's face.

"Mr. Lord is very sick."

Emily grasped at a chair. Everything went dark. A deathlike chill swept over her.

Tom Kelley, the hired man, had just come into the house and Emily ran to him, putting her head against his rough blue jacket.

"He will be better." Tom tried to comfort her. "I don't want to see you cry, Miss Emily." For Tom, like the other hired men and like Maggie Maher, the maid, was tenderly protective toward her.

From that moment on Emily lived in fear of losing Otis Lord. The same year he was taken ill, she lost her mother.

Seven years as her nurse had given Emily sympathy for her mother in place of pity. She had come to appreciate the deep love Mrs. Dickinson had felt for her husband.

Now only the two sisters and their servant Maggie occupied the spacious house. They continued to dress in the style of their girlhood. Vinnie had become something of a village character. Like Emily, she could be witty and amusing, but she was sharp-tongued and afraid of nobody. "With such a sister, I am well protected," Emily said.

Under Austin's direction trees and shrubs had sprung up around the college buildings; the village green had been drained and planted with elms. He was college treasurer, he served on town committees, and he was constantly making new friends.

In her own way, Emily struck up new friendships, too. On the Amherst College teaching staff was a young professor named Todd. Austin and Sue were enthusiastic about David Todd and his beautiful, accomplished wife, Mabel. The Todds were equally enthusiastic about the Dickinsons.

Soon after her arrival in Amherst, Mabel Todd began to hear about Austin's remarkable sister, who never went out and saw few people who called. When Vinnie invited the Todds to the brick house, she hoped for a glimpse of Emily.

After the first visit, however, Mabel Todd became used

to playing the piano and singing in the parlor, with Emily a "spot of white" in the hall outside.

At the end of such a recital, Emily would send in a poem, with sherry, cake, or a flower on a silver tray.

"I did not need to see her," Mabel Todd said. "Her personality was vibrant in her voice." She made Emily a painting of Indian pipe flowers, which was promptly hung in her room.

"I cannot make an Indian Pipe," Emily wrote in a note of thanks, "but please accept a Humming Bird." She enclosed a poem, describing not the bird itself, but its speed, its color, and the flowers tumbled by its flight.

> *A Route of Evanescence*
> *With a revolving Wheel—*
> *A resonance of Emerald—*
> *A Rush of Cochineal—*
> *And every Blossom on the Bush*
> *Adjusts its tumbled Head—*
> *The mail from Tunis, probably,*
> *An easy Morning's Ride—*

Poems like this convinced Mabel Todd that Emily Dickinson was a genius. She began to write in her diary many details of Emily's life that would otherwise be unknown.

Unable to face the parents, Emily made friends with their little daughter, Millicent. "To see her is a Picture," she said. "To hear her is a Tune."

"Front door callers" asking for Emily were told by

Maggie Maher that she was out, despite the well-known fact that she never left the grounds.

"Back door" callers fared better. Emily was quite willing to talk to tramps who came asking for food, to gypsies, and Indian women who came selling baskets.

Children might even be asked into the green-walled kitchen. There Emily would give them fresh-baked cookies, listen to their secrets, and say things that made their eyes widen. "My dears," she said once, "if the butcher boy called I should have to jump into the flour barrel."

At about this time Emily wrote the poem below:

From all the Jails the Boys and Girls
Ecstatically leap—
Beloved only Afternoon
That Prison doesn't keep—

They storm the Earth and Stun the Air,
A Mob of solid Bliss—
Alas—that Frowns should lie in wait
For such a Foe as this—

Though children were more likely than grownups to see her in person, even to them Emily was a mysterious figure.

One summer afternoon Austin's two older children, Ned and Martha Dickinson, were playing on the lawn with friends when suddenly a window above them opened. The glimpse of a white dress told them it was

Emily. As they watched, a basket came slowly down-ward on the end of a rope. The children pounced on it, finding, to their delight, four beautiful cakes of golden gingerbread.

No child who saw Emily in person ever forgot it. The grownups were always so curious about her. "What did she look like?" they would ask. "What did she say?"

Mac Jenkins remembered, even after he was grown up, seeing her once in her garden. "She was beautiful, dressed in white, with soft fiery brown eyes and a mass of auburn hair . . . cutting a few choice buds, she bade me take them, with her love, to my mother. . . . To have seen 'Miss Emily' was an event, and I ran home with a feeling of great importance to carry her message."

For her nephew Ned, who suffered from epilepsy, Emily felt a special tenderness. But of Austin's three chil-dren Gilbert, with his high spirits and enthusiasm, was her favorite. She repeated his remarks in letters and conspired with him against the world of grownups at times, espe-cially if he begged her, "Don't tell, Aunt Emily."

Once Gilbert held a little sale, and was asked what he planned to do with all the money. "Give half to the col-lege and half to the cat," he promptly answered. "When you grow up you'll be college treasurer like your father and grandfather," the grownups told him in amusement.

Then, one day when Gilbert was eight years old, play-ing with a friend in a mudhole, he contracted typhoid fever. In three days he was dead.

Emily never recovered from the shock. She had ner-vous prostration, her doctor told her.

Five months later, in March 1884, Judge Otis Lord died. By the following winter Emily was suffering from a serious kidney disease. Pain, fever, and weakness kept her in bed for months, with Vinnie her devoted nurse.

Her friends were still her "estate." As soon as she improved a little, she sat up to write notes to Thomas Higginson and others. Someone had given her a haunting story, *Called Back*, which she described in a letter to her cousins Loo and Fanny.

Spring arrived. The crocuses had blossomed and the daffodils were growing tall when she wrote to an aunt who was also ill, "Let us take hands and recover."

But in May, Louisa and Fanny Norcross received this note:

> Little Cousins,
> Called back—
> Emily.

After writing it, Emily fell asleep and then into a coma. A few days later, on May 15, 1886, she died.

In one of her poems Emily had written:

> *The Poets light but Lamps—*
> *Themselves—go out—*

In the bottom drawer of her cherry bureau were hundreds of other poems. Before she died Emily asked Lavinia to burn the many letters she had received and saved. She said nothing about her poems.

Lavinia was determined to see them published, and Mabel Todd agreed to help. Consulting with Thomas Wentworth Higginson, Mrs. Todd selected 115 poems and found a Boston firm willing to publish them if the family paid part of the cost.

When the poems appeared four years later, it was a literary event. The first book of poems was soon followed by two others and by a volume of Emily's letters.

From time to time during the next forty years, several more books of poems appeared, some edited by Emily's niece Martha, and one by Mabel Todd and her daughter Millicent. Finally ownership of the literary estate was transferred to Harvard University, which issued a complete collection of the poems and a collection of letters. For Emily Dickinson was a major American poet.

Selected Poems by Emily Dickinson

Dear March—Come in—
How glad I am—
I hoped for you before—

Put down your Hat—
You must have walked—
How out of Breath you are—
Dear March, how are you, and the Rest—
Did you leave Nature well—
Oh March, Come right up stairs with me—
I have so much to tell—

I got your Letter, and the Birds—
The Maples never knew that you were coming—till I
  called
I declare—how Red their Faces grew—
But March, forgive me—and
All those Hills you left for me to Hue—
There was no Purple suitable—
You took it all with you—

Who knocks? That April.
Lock the Door—
I will not be pursued—
He stayed away a Year to call
When I am occupied—
But trifles look so trivial
As soon as you have come

That Blame is just as dear as Praise
And Praise as mere as Blame—

A soft Sea washed around the House
A Sea of Summer Air
And rose and fell the magic Planks
That sailed without a care—
For Captain was the Butterfly
For Helmsman was the Bee
And an entire universe
For the delighted crew.

The morns are meeker than they were—
The nuts are getting brown—
The berry's cheek is plumper—
The Rose is out of town.

The Maple wears a gayer scarf—
The field a scarlet gown—
Lest I should be old fashioned
I'll put a trinket on.

I like to see it lap the Miles—
And lick the Valleys up—
And stop to feed itself at Tanks—
And then—prodigious step

Around a Pile of Mountains—
And supercilious peer
In Shanties—by the sides of Roads—
And then a Quarry pare

To fit its Ribs
And crawl between
Complaining all the while
In horrid—hooting stanza—
Then chase itself down Hill—

And neigh like Boanerges—
Then—punctual as a Star
Stop—docile and omnipotent
At its own stable door—

This—is the land—the Sunset washes—
These—are the Banks of the Yellow Sea—
Where it rose—or whither it rushes—
These—are the Western Mystery!

Night after Night
Her purple traffic
Strews the landing with Opal Bales—
Merchantmen—poise upon Horizons—
Dip—and vanish like Orioles!

Some keep the Sabbath going to Church—
I keep it, staying at Home—
With a Bobolink for a Chorister—
And an Orchard, for a Dome—

Some keep the Sabbath in Surplice—
I just wear my Wings—
And instead of tolling the Bell, for Church,
Our little Sexton—sings.

God preaches, a noted Clergyman—
And the sermon is never long,
So instead of getting to Heaven, at last—
I'm going, all along.

I started Early—Took my Dog—
And visited the Sea—
The Mermaids in the Basement
Came out to look at me—

And Frigates—in the Upper Floor
Extended Hempen Hands—
Presuming Me to be a Mouse—
Aground—upon the Sands—

But no Man moved Me—till the Tide
Went past my simple Shoe—
And past my Apron—and my Belt
And past my Bodice—too—

And made as He would eat me up—
As wholly as a Dew
Upon a Dandelion's Sleeve—
And then—I started—too—

And He—He followed—close behind—
I felt His Silver Heel
Upon my Ankle—Then my Shoes
Would overflow with Pearl—

Until We met the Solid Town—
No One He seemed to know—
And bowing—with a Mighty look—
At me—The Sea withdrew—

A Bird came down the Walk—
He did not know I saw—
He bit an Angleworm in halves
And ate the fellow, raw,

And then he drank a Dew
From a convenient Grass—
And then hopped sidewise to the Wall
To let a Beetle pass—

He glanced with rapid eyes
That hurried all around—
They looked like frightened Beads, I thought—
He stirred his Velvet Head

Like one in danger, Cautious,
I offered him a Crumb
And he unrolled his feathers
And rowed him softer home—

Than Oars divide the Ocean,
Too silver for a seam—
Or Butterflies, off Banks of Noon
Leap, plashless as they swim.

How happy is the little Stone
That rambles in the Road alone,
And doesn't care about Careers
And Exigencies never fears—
Whose Coat of elemental Brown
A passing Universe put on,
And independent as the Sun
Associates or glows alone,
Fulfilling absolute Decree
In casual simplicity—

Will there really be a "Morning"?
Is there such a thing as "Day"?
Could I see it from the mountains
If I were as tall as they?

Has it feet like Water lilies?
Has it feathers like a Bird?
Is it brought from famous countries
Of which I have never heard?

Oh some Scholar! Oh some Sailor!
Oh some Wise Man from the skies!
Please to tell a little Pilgrim
Where the place called "Morning" lies!

Bee! I'm expecting you!
Was saying Yesterday
To Somebody you know
That you were due—

The Frogs got Home last Week—
Are settled, and at work—
Birds, mostly back—
The Clover warm and thick—

You'll get my Letter by
The seventeenth; Reply
Or better, be with me—
Yours, Fly.

To fight aloud, is very brave—
But gallanter, *I know*
Who charge within the bosom
The Cavalry of Woe—

Who win, and nations do not see—
Who fall—and none observe—
Whose dying eyes, no Country
Regards with patriot love—

We trust, in plumed procession
For such, the Angels go—
Rank after Rank, with even feet—
And Uniforms of Snow.

The Brain—is wider than the Sky—
For—put them side by side—
The one the other will contain
With ease—and You—beside—

The Brain is deeper than the sea—
For—hold them—Blue to Blue—
The one the other will absorb—
As Sponges—Buckets—do—

The Brain is just the weight of God—
For—Heft them—Pound for Pound—
And they will differ—if they do—
As Syllable from Sound—

The Soul selects her own Society—
Then—shuts the Door—
To her divine Majority—
Present no more—

Unmoved—she notes the Chariots—pausing—
At her low Gate—
Unmoved—an Emperor be kneeling
Upon her Mat—

I've known her—from an ample nation—
Choose One—
Then—close the Valves of her attention—
Like Stone—

I felt a Funeral, in my Brain,
And Mourners to and fro
Kept treading—treading—till it seemed
That Sense was breaking through—

And when they all were seated,
A Service, like a Drum—
Kept beating—beating—till I thought
My Mind was going numb—

And then I heard them lift a Box
And creak across my Soul
With those same Boots of Lead, again,
Then Space—began to toll,

As all the Heavens were a Bell,
And Being, but an Ear,
And I, and Silence, some strange Race
Wrecked, solitary, here—

And then a Plank in Reason, broke,
And I dropped down, and down—
And hit a World, at every plunge,
And Finished knowing—then—

"Hope" is the thing with feathers—
That perches in the soul—
And sings the tune without the words—
And never stops—at all—

And sweetest—in the Gale—is heard—
And sore must be the storm—
That could abash the little Bird
That kept so many warm—

I've heard it in the chillest land—
And on the strangest Sea—
Yet, never, in Extremity,
It asked a crumb—of Me.

Safe in their Alabaster Chambers—
Untouched by Morning
And untouched by Noon—
Sleep the meek members of the Resurrection—
Rafter of satin,
And Roof of stone.

Light laughs the breeze
In her Castle above them—
Babbles the Bee in a stolid Ear,
Pipe the Sweet Birds in ignorant cadence—
Ah, what sagacity perished here!

VERSION OF 1859

Safe in their Alabaster Chambers—
Untouched by Morning—
And untouched by Noon—
Lie the meek members of the Resurrection—
Rafter of Satin—and Roof of Stone!

Grand go the Years—in the Crescent—above them—
Worlds scoop their Arcs—
And Firmaments—row—
Diadems—drop—and Doges—surrender—
Soundless as dots—on a Disc of Snow—

VERSION OF 1861

I'll tell you how the Sun rose—
A Ribbon at a time—
The Steeples swam in Amethyst—
The news, like Squirrels, ran—
The Hills untied their Bonnets—
The Bobolinks—begun—
Then I said softly to myself—
"That must have been the Sun"!
But how he set—I know not—
There seemed a purple stile
That little Yellow boys and girls
Were climbing all the while—
Till when they reached the other side,
A Dominie in Gray—
Put gently up the evening Bars—
And led the flock away—

A narrow Fellow in the Grass
Occasionally rides—
You may have met Him—did you not
His notice sudden is—

The Grass divides as with a Comb—
A spotted shaft is seen—
And then it closes at your feet
And opens further on—

He likes a Boggy Acre
A Floor too cool for Corn—
Yet when a Boy, and Barefoot—
I more than once at Noon
Have passed, I thought, a Whip lash
Unbraiding in the Sun
When stooping to secure it
It wrinkled, and was gone—

Several of Nature's People
I know, and they know me—
I feel for them a transport
Of cordiality—

But never met this Fellow
Attended, or alone
Without a tighter breathing
And Zero at the Bone—

This is my letter to the World
That never wrote to Me—
The simple News that Nature told—
With tender Majesty

Her Message is committed
To Hands I cannot see—
For love of Her—Sweet—countrymen—
Judge tenderly—of Me

Because I could not stop for Death—
He kindly stopped for me—
The Carriage held but just Ourselves—
And Immortality.

We slowly drove—He knew no haste
And I had put away
My labor and my leisure too,
For His Civility—

We passed the School, where Children strove
At Recess—in the Ring—
We passed the Fields of Gazing Grain—
We passed the Setting Sun—

Or rather—He passed Us—
The Dews drew quivering and chill—
For only Gossamer, my Gown—
My Tippet—only Tulle—

We paused before a House that seemed
A Swelling of the Ground—
The Roof was scarcely visible—
The Cornice—in the Ground—

Since then—'tis Centuries—and yet
Feels shorter than the Day
I first surmised the Horses' Heads
Were toward Eternity—

Success is counted sweetest
By those who ne'er succeed.
To comprehend a nectar
Requires sorest need.

Not one of all the purple Host
Who took the Flag today
Can tell the definition
So clear of Victory

As he defeated—dying—
On whose forbidden ear
The distant strains of triumph
Burst agonized and clear!

New feet within my garden go—
New fingers stir the sod—
A Troubadour upon the Elm
Betrays the solitude.

New children play upon the green—
New Weary sleep below—
And still the pensive Spring returns—
And still the punctual snow!

For Further Reading

Gemming, Elizabeth. *Huckleberry Hill: Child Life in Old New England*. New York: Thomas Y. Crowell Company, 1968. A season by season chronicle of life in a 19th century New England town or village, with many photographs of paintings and engravings showing people, interiors and landscapes, as well as photographs of tools, toys, samplers, etc.

Stowe, Harriet Beecher. *Uncle Tom's Cabin*. There are many editions, some with illustrations. The famous pre-Civil War story of the cruel treatment of an aged slave by a white overseer. First published in 1852, the book aroused intense feeling against slavery in the North, turning the quarrel with the South into a moral as well as political one.

Wood, James Playsted. *The People of Concord*. New York: The Seabury Press, 1970. Contains a chapter on Ralph Waldo Emerson, whose philosophy of trusting one's own instincts and of being one's self appealed so much to Emily Dickinson.

MORE ADVANCED READING

Fisher, Aileen, and Rabe, Olive. *We Dickinsons*. New York: Atheneum, 1965. A portrait of Emily Dickinson from her brother Austin's point of view, told in the first person, with good examples of the poet's wit but no sampling of the poetry.

Longsworth, Polly. *Emily Dickinson: Her Letter to the World*. New York: Thomas Y. Crowell Company, 1965. A splendid biography, interspersed with samples of poetry, for the older, more advanced, or "special" reader.

Meltzer, Milton. *Tongue of Flame: The Life of Lydia Maria Child*. New York: Thomas Y. Crowell Company, 1965. The story of the abolitionist and women's rights advocate whose ideas so impressed Emily Dickinson.

Meyer, Howard N. *Colonel of the Black Regiment: The Life of Thomas Wentworth Higginson*. New York: W. W. Norton & Company, 1967. The story of Emily's "tutor" and of the Union army's first official regiment of ex-slaves, which he commanded.

Sources

THE FOLLOWING books, as well as those previously listed, were helpful to the author:

Anderson, Charles R. *Emily Dickinson's Poetry: Stairway of Surprise*. New York: Holt, Rinehart and Winston, 1960.

Bingham, Millicent Todd. *Ancestor's Brocades*. New York: Harper & Brothers, 1945.

Bingham, Millicent Todd. *Emily Dickinson's Home*. New York: Harper & Brothers, 1955.

Blake, Caesar R., and Wells, Carlton F., editors. *The Recognition of Emily Dickinson*. Ann Arbor: The University of Michigan Press, 1964.

Higgins, David. *Portrait of Emily Dickinson: The Poet and Her Prose*. New Brunswick: Rutgers University Press, 1967.

Jenkins, MacGregor. *Emily Dickinson: Friend and Neighbor*. Boston: Little, Brown and Company, 1930.

Johnson, Thomas H. *Emily Dickinson: An Interpretive*

Biography. Cambridge: Harvard University Press, 1955.

Johnson, Thomas H., editor. *The Letters of Emily Dickinson*. Cambridge: The Belknap Press of Harvard University Press. 3 vols. 1958.

Leyda, Jay. *The Years and Hours of Emily Dickinson*. New Haven: Yale University Press. 2 vols. 1960.

Wells, Anna Mary. *Dear Preceptor: The Life and Times of Thomas Wentworth Higginson*. Boston: Houghton Mifflin Company, 1963.

Whicher, George F., editor. *Remembrance of Amherst: An Undergraduate's Diary*. New York: Columbia University Press, 1946.

Whicher, George F. *This Was a Poet: A Critical Biography of Emily Dickinson*. New York: Charles Scribner's Sons, 1938.

Index of Poems by First Lines

"Arcturus" is his other name (*last two stanzas*), 29
Because I could not stop for Death, 117
Bee! I'm expecting you!, 107
A Bird came down the Walk, 104
The Brain—is wider than the Sky, 109
Dear March—Come in, 97
From all the Jails the Boys and Girls, 90
"Hope" is the thing with feathers, 112
How happy is the little Stone, 105
How still the Bells in Steeples stand, 45
I felt a Funeral, in my Brain, 111
I like to see it lap the Miles, 100
I'll tell you how the Sun rose, 114
I'm nobody! Who are you?, 72–73
I never hear the word "escape," 53
I started Early—Took my Dog, 103
I taste a liquor never brewed (*first two lines*), 61
The morns are meeker than they were, 99
The Mushroom is the Elf of Plants (*first stanza*), 20
A narrow Fellow in the Grass, 115
New feet within my garden go, 119
Of all the Sounds despatched abroad (*first stanza*), 68
The pattern of the sun, 45
The Poets light but Lamps (*first two lines*), 92

A Route of Evanescence, 89
Safe in their Alabaster Chambers: *version of 1859*, 113; *version of 1861*, 113
The Show is not the Show, 35
A soft Sea washed around the House, 98
Some keep the Sabbath going to Church, 102
The Soul selects her own Society, 110
South Winds jostle them, 67–68
Success is counted sweetest, 118
There came a Day at Summer's full (*first stanza*), 68
This is my letter to the World, 116
This—is the land—the Sunset washes, 101
To fight aloud, is very brave, 108
To make a prairie it takes a clover and one bee, 58
To see the Summer Sky, 81
We introduce ourselves, 46
Will there really be a "Morning"?, 106
A word is dead, 25

Index

Abolitionists, 41
Alcott, Louisa May, 84
Amherst Academy, 23–27
Amherst College, 18
  Austin Dickinson as treasurer of, 88
  Commencement Week at, 45–46
Amherst (Massachusetts), 14
Arch Street Presbyterian Church, 48
Atlantic Monthly, 63–64, 70, 79

Bowles, Samuel, 60, 63, 71, 81
  death of, 82–83
  as editor of the *Daily Springfield Republican*, 55–56

Carlo (Emily Dickinson's dog), 53–54, 74
Child, Lydia Maria, 41
Childhood of Emily Dickinson, 13–29
Children, Emily Dickinson and, 90–91
Civil War, 61
Colonel of the Black Regiment: The Life of Thomas Wentworth Higginson (Meyer), 122
Commencement Week at Amherst College, 45–46

Daily Springfield Republican, see Springfield Republican
Death of Emily Dickinson, 92–93
Dickinson, Austin (brother), 23, 43–44, 61–62, 84, 88
  childhood of, 13–15, 17–19
  marriage to Sue Gilbert of, 50
Dickinson, Edward (father), 29, 30
  childhood of Emily Dickinson and, 14–16, 18

  death of, 80–81
  election to Congress of, 46, 78
Dickinson, Edward (son of Austin), 61–62, 90, 91
Dickinson, Gilbert (son of Austin), 84, 91
Dickinson, Lavinia (sister), 30–31, 84
  childhood of, 13–15, 17–19, 25
  death of Emily and, 91–92
Dickinson, Martha (daughter of Austin), 90–91
Dickinson, Sue, *see* Gilbert, Sue
Dickinson, Vinnie, *see* Dickinson, Lavinia

Education of Emily Dickinson, 23–27
  at Mount Holyoke, 30–39
Emerson, Ralph Waldo, 79, 84
Emily Dickinson: Her Letter to the World (Longsworth), 122

Fisher, Aileen, 122
Fort Sumter, 61

Garrison, William Lloyd, 41
Gemming, Elizabeth, 121
Gilbert, Mattie, 49
Gilbert, Sue, 58–60
  children born to, 61–62
  family strain and, 84
  marriage to Austin Dickinson of, 49–51

Harvard University, 93
Hawthorne, Nathaniel, 79
Higginson, Thomas Wentworth, 93
  correspondence with Emily and, 65–70, 72–73, 74–75

as editor of the *Atlantic Monthly*, 63–64

meeting with Emily and, 76–78

Holland, Josiah, 55

Howland, William, 44

Huckleberry Hill: Child Life in Old New England (Gemming), 121

Humphrey, Leonard, 47

Imperfect rhyme, 69

Jackson, Helen Hunt, 84–85

  Ramona, 81–82

Jenkins, Mac, 91

Kelly, Tom, 87

Liberator, The, 41

Lincoln, Abraham, 61

Longsworth, Polly, 122

Lord, Otis, 87–88

  death of, 92

  Emily Dickinson and, 83–85

Lyon, Mary, 31–33, 36

Mack, Deacon, 14

Maher, Maggie, 76, 88, 89–90

Meltzer, Milton, 122

Meyer, Howard N., 122

Mount Holyoke Female Seminary, 30–39

Newton, Benjamin, 41–42, 45

  death of, 47

Norcross, Emily, 31, 37, 38, 47

  death of, 47

Norcross, Fanny, 73, 92

Norcross, Louisa, 73, 92

Orthodox Congregational church, 28

People of Concord (Wood), 121–22

Poetry, Emily Dickinson's description of, 78

Rabe, Olive, 122

Ramona (Jackson), 81–82

Religion, Emily Dickinson and, 27–29, 33, 34, 36–38, 48

  Benjamin Newton and, 41–43

  at Mount Holyoke, 33, 36–38

Root, Abiah, 25, 29, 33, 44

Slavery, 41

Springfield Republican, 47, 62–63, 74

  Samuel Bowles and, 55–56

  Howland and valentine of Emily Dickinson, 44

Star of the West (ship), 61

Stowe, Harriet Beecher, 46, 121

Suspended rhyme, 69

Todd, David, 88

Todd, Mabel, 88, 93

Todd, Millicent, 89, 93

Tongue of Flame: The Life of Lydia Maria Child (Meltzer), 122

Transcendentalism, 42–43

Uncle Tom's Cabin (Stowe), 46, 121

Unitarianism, 41

Wadsworth, Charles, 48, 54, 60, 63

  death of, 85–86

  meeting with Emily Dickinson and, 56–57

We Dickinsons (Fisher and Rabe), 122

Whittier, John Greenleaf, 84

Williston Seminary, 23

Women's rights, 41

Wood, James Playsted, 121–22